TWEEN BIBLE PUZZLES

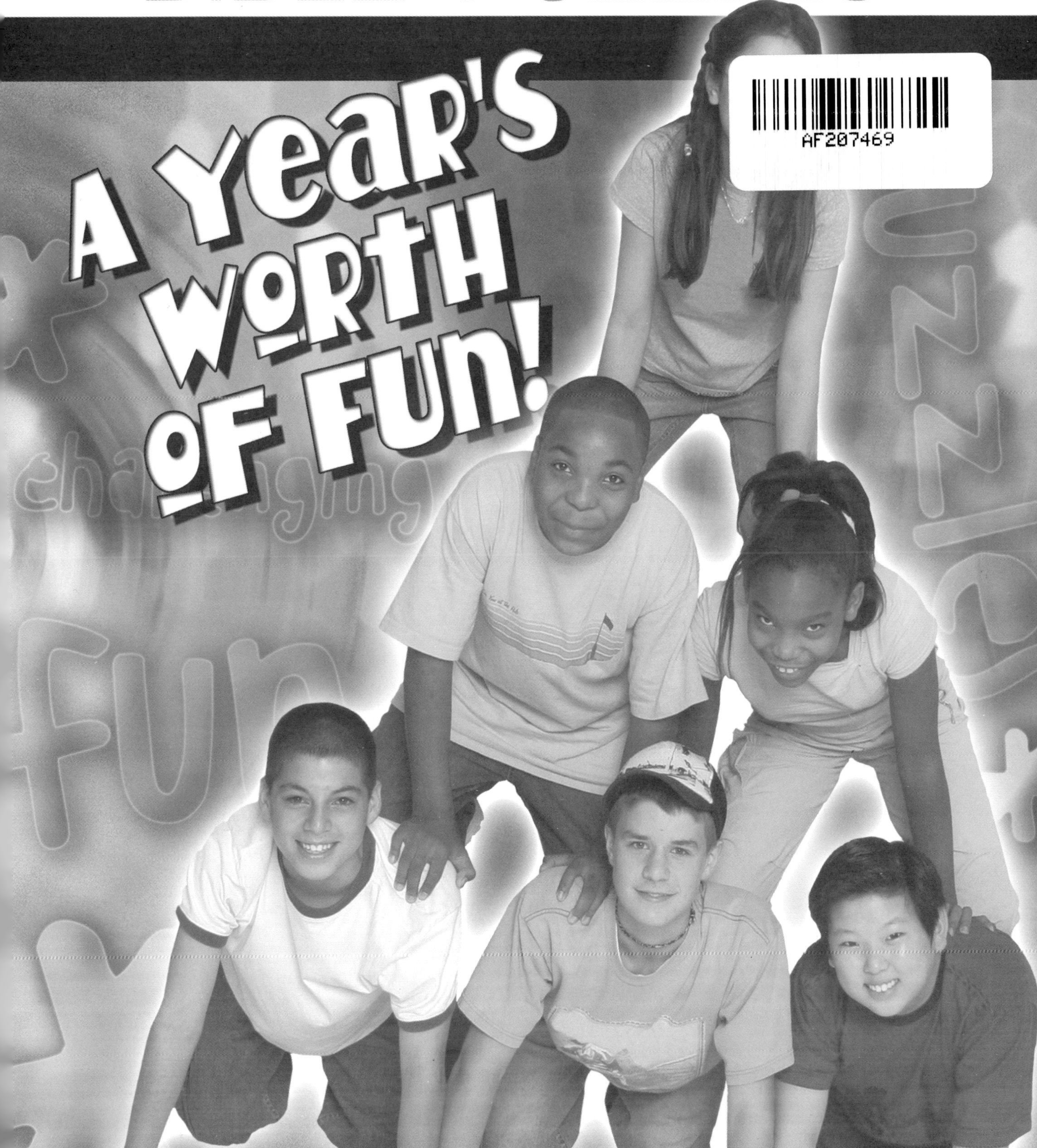

Tween Bible Puzzles:
A Year's Worth of Fun

Writer/Editor: Marcia Stoner
Designer: Keitha Vincent
Cover Photo: Ron Benedict
Additional Credits: p. 144.

ISBN 0-687-49731-0

05 06 07 08 09 10 11 12 13 14 — 10 9 8 7 6 5 4 3 2 1

Manufactured in the United States of America

Contents

HOW TO USE THIS BOOK

For arrival (or additional) activities for any curriculum
• These puzzles can be used for arrival activities to supplement any Bible curriculum. Use the Topical and Scripture Indexes to find the puzzle that applies to what your class is studying.

For a nine-month Bible survey
• If you are doing a school-year overview of the Bible with your tweens, you will find puzzles for most of the topics you will cover. You would mainly use the puzzles for the first thirty-nine weeks, which are labeled 1 through 39B (two puzzles per week).

For a twelve-month Bible survey
• If you are doing a twelve-month overview of the Bible with your tweens, you will find puzzles for most of the topics you will cover. The additional summer puzzles beginning on page 89 may be used in two ways:

1. Strictly for additional topics for summer. (Because so many tweens are in and out of class in the summer months, you probably will not want to leave most of the New Testament work to summer.)

2. At the appropriate place where they fall within the Bible. If you are unsure where that would be, see the Scripture index on pages 142-143. Those Scriptures with ** preceding them in the index are the additional summer puzzles. They are listed in the index in the order where the Scriptures they cover appear in the Bible.

For _Exploring Faith: Tweens in Transition_ Users
• If you are using the _Exploring Faith: Tweens in Transition_ Sunday school curriculum for the year 2005–2006, you will find two puzzles for each session in the exact order of the lessons. You may use one or both of the puzzles to supplement your lessons, or you may wish to send one puzzle home each week with your tweens.
• Some of the puzzles are to help you bridge some stories not included in the curriculum for this year (such as the Baptism of Jesus). The puzzle can be used to include the connecting story.

The Question
• There is a discussion question on each puzzle page. You may want to ask your tweens the question as part of your class time. There is no specified answer for the discussion question. The question is designed to facilitate discussion or to make your tweens think.

From Creation Through the Prophets

Serpent in the Garden

There are fifteen words from Genesis 3 in this word search. Circle the words and list them below. You will find words in the puzzle forward, backward, and diagonally. (Hint: There are some words in the puzzle that are NOT in Genesis 3. They don't count.)

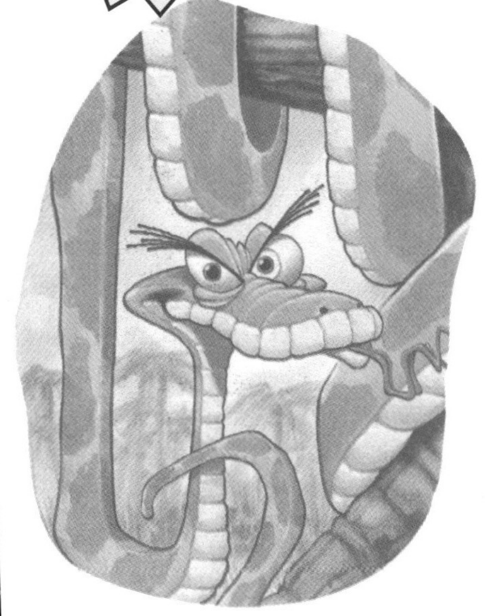

H	E	M	C	O	M	M	A	N	D	E	D
U	S	E	C	E	P	M	P	N	E	C	G
S	O	O	L	L	L	I	F	E	M	T	A
B	X	P	O	D	E	X	P	I	N	R	R
A	E	E	T	D	V	V	E	E	S	E	D
N	N	N	H	I	I	G	P	G	O	D	E
D	B	E	E	M	L	R	O	O	B	E	N
F	E	D	D	S	E	D	L	O	G	A	S
D	U	S	T	S	H	I	D	L	I	T	E
K	N	O	W	I	N	G	W	O	M	A	N

________________ ________________ ________________

________________ ________________ ________________

________________ ________________ ________________

________________ ________________ ________________

________________ ________________ ________________

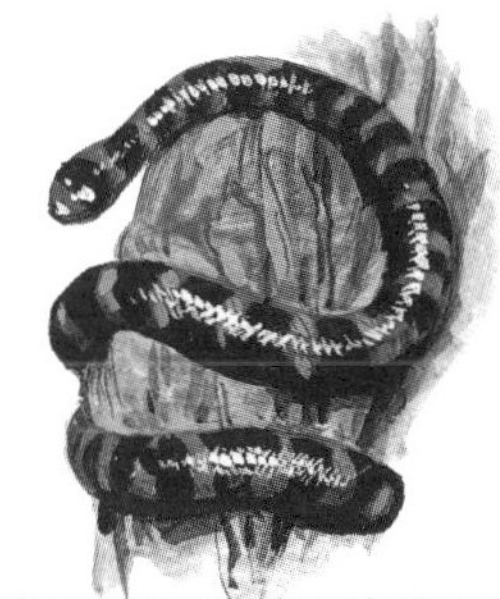

Curious Caleb's Confused Creation

Curious Caleb's computer has crashed. This means that Caleb has to reorganize his notes. Help Caleb answer these questions, many of which are out of order. You may need to refer to the first three chapters of Genesis to see if you are right.

1. On what day was humankind created?

2. Humankind was given responsibility over all that lives on the earth. What is this responsibility called?

3. Adam and Eve were told NOT to do something. What was it they were told not to do?

4. Who told Eve it was okay to do it?

5. Why was it wrong for Adam and Eve to do what they did?

6. Were the sun and the moon created before or after the creatures that creep on the earth?

7. What did God do on the seventh day?

8. Who gave the animals names?

9. What was the very first thing God created?

10. What are the first words that the Bible records God as saying?

Old Testament Puzzles, © 2005 Abingdon Press

WHO? WHAT? HOW?

Can you figure out the answers to these questions about two brothers named Cain and Abel? Try doing it without looking at the Bible. After you've answered as many questions as you can, read Genesis 4:1-16 and score yourself.

1. Which brother was older, Cain or Abel?

2. What did each brother do on the farm?

3. Many translations of the Bible use the word *countenance* in Genesis 4:5. *Countenance* means the expressions of the face. What might it mean that Cain's countenance "fell"?

4. Why was Cain angry?
   A. Abel was mean and teased Cain.
   B. Abel cheated Cain.
   C. Cain was jealous because God liked Abel's offering better than Cain's.
   D. We don't know.

5. What did Cain do to Abel?

6. What was the first thing God said to Cain after Cain killed Abel?

If you want to know Cain's response to God, work puzzle 2B before you read the story from the Bible.

Questioning Alphabet

Solve the missing-alphabet puzzle to discover Cain's response to God.
Find the letter that is missing from each line and write it on a line below
in order. Read Genesis 4:9 to see if you got it right.

BCDEFGHIJKLMNOPQRSTUVWXYZ
ABCDEFGHIJKLNOPQRSTUVWXYZ

ABCDEFGHJKLMNOPQRSTUVWXYZ

ABCDEFGHIJKLNOPQRSTUVWXYZ
ABCDEFGHIJKLMNOPQRSTUVWXZ

ACDEFGHIJKLMNOPQRSTUVWXYZ
ABCDEFGHIJKLMNOPQSTUVWXYZ
ABCDEFGHIJKLMNPQRSTUVWXYZ
ABCDEFGHIJKLMNOPQRSUVWXYZ
ABCDEFGIJKLMNOPQRSTUVWXYZ
ABCDFGHIJKLMNOPQRSTUVWXYZ
ABCDEFGHIJKLMNOPQSTUVWXYZ
ABCDEFGHIJKLMNOPQRTUVWXYZ

ABCDEFGHIJLMNOPQRSTUVWXYZ
ABCDFGHIJKLMNOPQRSTUVWXYZ
ABCDFGHIJKLMNOPQRSTUVWXYZ
ABCDEFGHIJKLMNOQRSTUVWXYZ
ABCDFGHIJKLMNOPQRSTUVWXYZ
ABCDEFGHIJKLMNOPQSTUVWXYZ

__ __ __ __ __ __

__ __ __ __ __ __ __ __

__ __ __ __ __ __ __ ?

TOWER OF WORDS

Read Genesis 11:1-9, then fill in the blanks using the words below.

Oh yes, by the way, just to make it a little more challenging, there are words listed that aren't used at all!

What did God do to the people of Babel? Why did God do it?

Now the whole ______________ had one ____________________

and the same ______________.

And the people of Babel said to one another, "Come, let us make ______________,

and ______________ them thoroughly."

And they had brick for ________________, and bitumen for ________________.

Then they said, "Come, let us __________ourselves a ____________ , and a

______________ with its top in the ________________, and let us make a

______________ for ourselves; otherwise we shall be ____________________

abroad upon the face of the whole earth."

---

bake	destroy	mortar	sky
bricks	driven	name	stone
build	earth	problem	tablets
burn	hammer	scattered	tower
city	heavens	sea	town
country	language	settled	words
	monument		

Tower of Babel

The people who were building the tower of Babel were scattered because the people focused on what they wanted and not what God wanted for them. A word of warning comes to us in Philippians 2:3a that we would be wise to heed. Follow the directions carefully to discover what it is. Check your answer in the Bible.

1. Cross out all the words that begin with "B."

2. Cross out all the words that end in "Y."

3. Cross out all words that are numbers.

4. Cross out all words that have double letters in them.

Why is it important to think about the reason we do things?

BIG TEN MANY DO WHY BELL SELL SIX NOTHING TEETH NOON BEFORE FROM

FOOTBALL TWO DELAY BEST BETTER SEE SELFISH FIVE ANY AMBITION

COOL BASKETBALL SPORTY OR TWELVE LOOK ONE BETWEEN CONCEIT

WEARY SEVENTEEN TOOL YESTERDAY BABY BEFORE EIGHTY DAY MOON

Write the words that remain in the box in order on the blanks below.

________ ________ ________ ________ ________ ________ ________

________ ________ ________ ________ ________ ________ ________

________ ________ ________ ________ ________.

12

MAP FOR PEACE

Read Genesis 12:10 and 13:1-18. Using the letters already in place as a guide, add the names of the locations vertically to their proper places on the puzzle. Then use a pen or pencil to trace this part of Abram's journey on the map.

Would it be difficult for you to give your brother or your cousin the first choice of two things you really like?

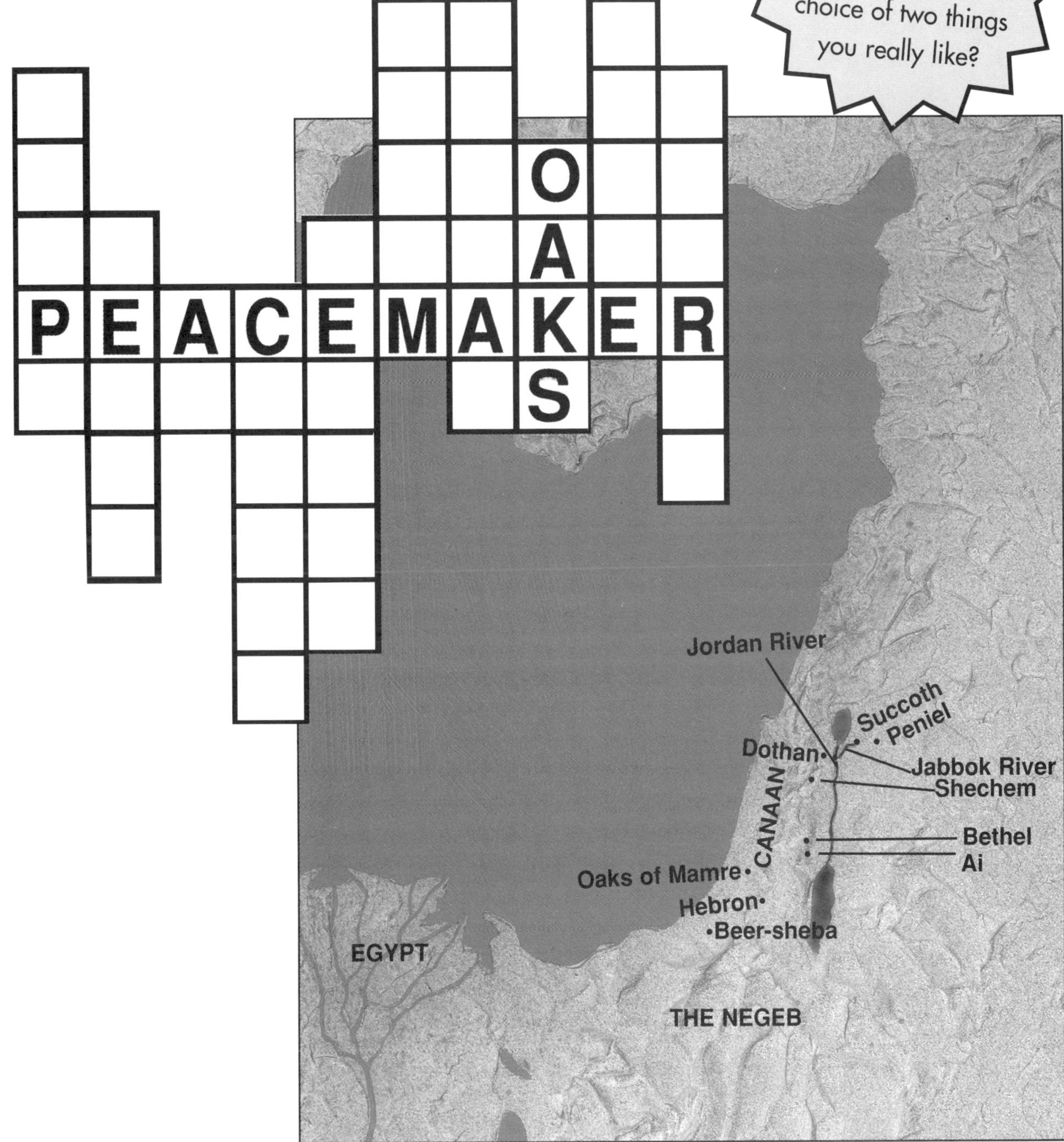

DECODE A BIBLE VERSE

Abram wanted to live peacefully with his nephew Lot, so Abram looked at a troublesome situation from his own point of view and from Lot's point of view. Alternate choosing a word from each silhouette to learn the words Abram spoke to Lot. Write your answer in the space below.

Left silhouette:

Let
be
strife
you
me
between
herders
my
for
are
Is
the
land
you
yourself
me
you
the
hand
I
go
the
or
you
the
hand
I
go
the

Right silhouette:

there
no
between
and
and
your
and
herders
we
kindred
not
whole
before
Separate
from
If
take
left
then
will
to
right
if
take
right
then
will
to
left

If you were given the first choice between two things, how would you make the choice?

Check your answer by reading Genesis 13:8-9.

Old Testament Puzzles, © 2005 Abingdon Press

A Proverb

There is a proverb that explains how Abraham acted when he (with a heavy heart) followed God's instructions concerning his young son, Isaac.

Why would God put Abraham to such a serious test?

In order to discover the proverb, circle the words in these locations:

1/A   1/F   1/I   2/C   2/E   3/G   3/J   4/E   4/J   5/I   6/A   6/F

7/A   8/D   8/H   8/J

	A	B	C	D	E	F	G	H	I	J
1	Lord	be	my	can	soul	rely	down	new	your	mine
2	mind	today	trust	yours	own	right	never	I	his	low
3	soon	know	care	love	all	soon	insight	on	an	in
4	very	heart	once	ever	do	should	would	my	own	with
5	little	know	see	what	others	to	be	and	and	truly
6	on	only	do	work	help	not	go	above	it	so
7	the	children	God	one	two	no	under	now	we	Jesus
8	choose	what	do	heart	so	come	to	all	my	your

Put the words you circled in the correct order to find Proverbs 3:5.

___ ___ ___ ___ ___ ___ ___ ___ ___ ___

___ ___ ___ ___ ___ ___ ____, ___ ___ ___

___ ___ ___ ___ ___ ___ ___ ___ ___

___ ___ ___ ___ ___.

Monotheism

When Abraham and Sarah lived, most people believed in many gods. They would pray to different gods to ask for different favors, such as rain for their crops or the ability to have children. The belief in many gods is called *polytheism*.

Monotheism is the belief in one God. The stories in Genesis tell us about people who came to understand that only one God is to be worshiped. Abraham and Sarah discovered some wonderful things about the one God. Complete the statements below to learn about some Old Testament verses that help us worship and obey the one God.

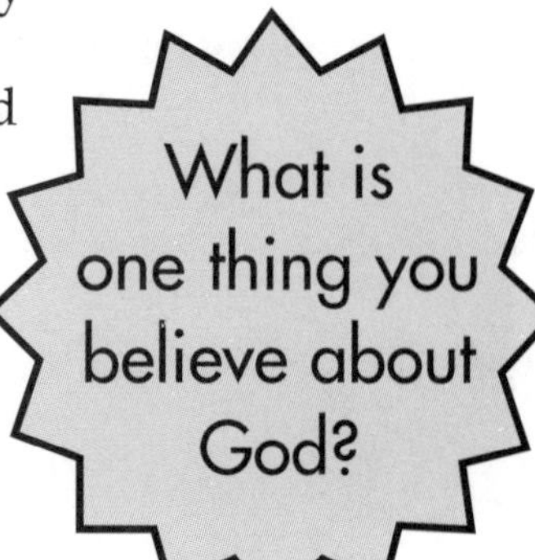

Make no _________________. (Exodus 20:4)

Obey God's _________________. (Deuteronomy 13:4)

No other _________________ are to be worshiped. (Exodus 20:3)

Only the _________________ is to be worshiped. (Deuteronomy 6:4)

Trust in the Lord, and do _________________. (Psalm 37:3)

Heaven and _________________ shall praise God. (Psalm 69:34)

Everlasting is God's _________________. (Psalm 145:13)

Incline your _________________ to God. (Joshua 24:23)

Salvation comes from God; whom shall I _________________? (Psalm 27:1)

Mighty and _________________ is the Lord. (Psalm 24:8)

The Not So Good Deal

Esau made a bad bargain in Genesis 25:29-34. Solve the puzzle below to discover what Esau sold and what he got in return.

Esau sold his ___ ___ ___ ___ ___ ___ ___ ___ ___ ___
　　　　　　　　1　2　3　4　5　6　7　8　9　10

for ___ ___ ___ ___.
　　11　12　13　14

1. Last letter of the eighteenth Old Testament book.

2. First letter of the twenty-third Old Testament book.

3. First letter of the last book of the Bible.

4. Fifth letter of the third Old Testament book.

5. Fourth letter of the sixth Old Testament book.

6. Sixth letter of the fifth Old Testament book.

7. First letter of the book of the Old Testament that comes after Song of Solomon.

8. First letter of the first Old Testament book.

9. Last letter of the eighth Old Testament book.

10. Third letter of the seventeenth Old Testament book.

11. First letter of the first Old Testament book that has a 1 in front of it.

12. Fourth letter of the fifth Old Testament book.

13. First letter of the second Old Testament book.

14. Last letter of the first book of the New Testament.

What's True? What's Not?

The story of how Jacob stole Esau's birthright is full of deception. The account of the story written below is also sometimes deceiving. Mark which statements are true and which are false so that you will know the truth of the story. Read Genesis 27:1–28:5.

1. The parents of Jacob and Esau were Abraham and Sarah. T F

2. Jacob and Esau were twins. T F

3. Esau was the older brother. T F

4. The older brother was the one who would inherit the blessing. T F

5. Jacob was told by a close friend how to deceive his father. T F

6. Jacob's father was almost blind, so Jacob put hairy skins on his arms so that his father would think he was Esau. T F

7. Jacob's father believed the deception right away. T F

8. Isaac gave Esau's blessing to Jacob. T F

9. Because of the stolen blessing, Esau got nothing. T F

10. Jacob lived happily ever after on the family estate. T F

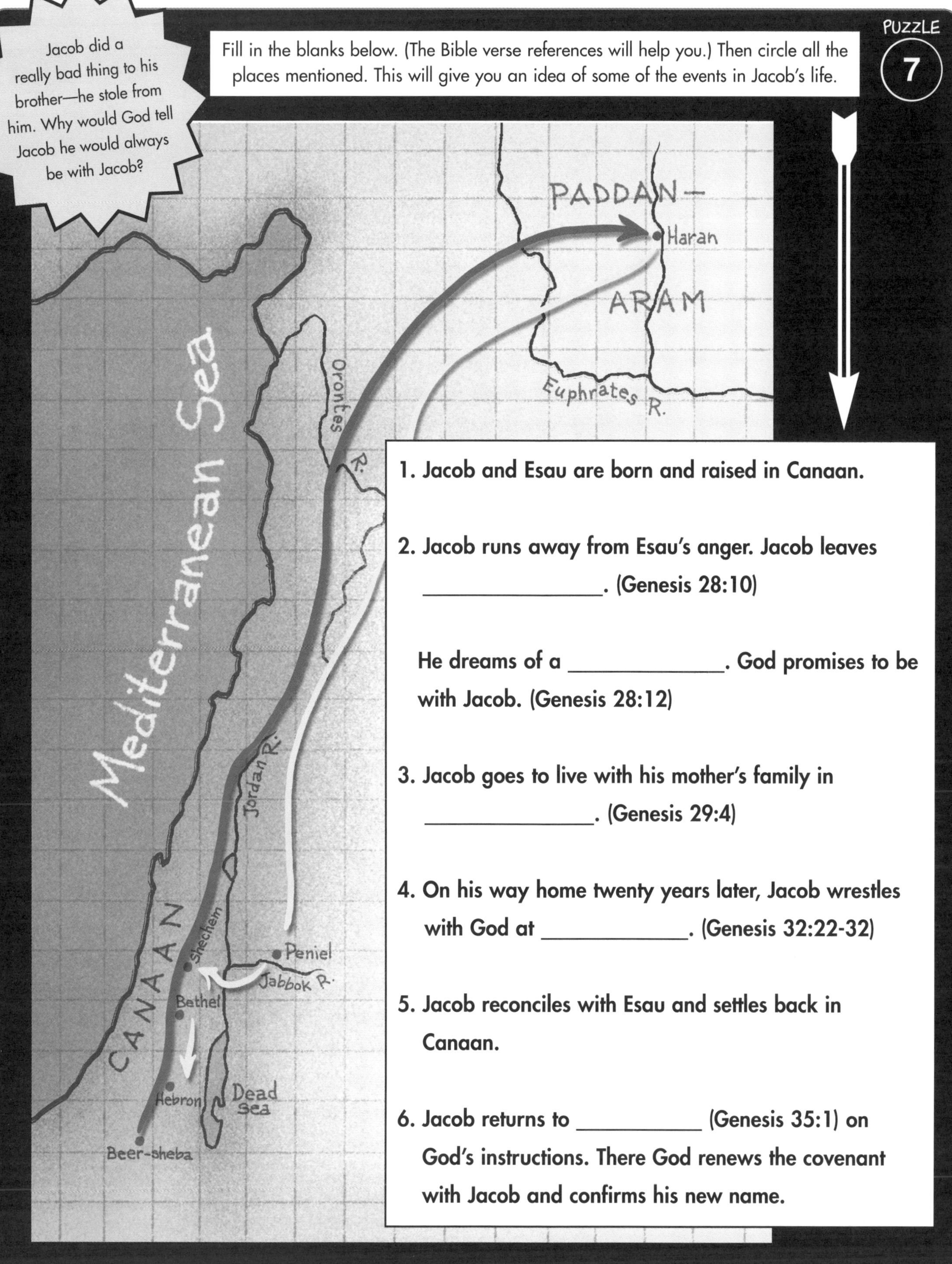

Fill in the blanks below. (The Bible verse references will help you.) Then circle all the places mentioned. This will give you an idea of some of the events in Jacob's life.

1. Jacob and Esau are born and raised in Canaan.

2. Jacob runs away from Esau's anger. Jacob leaves ________________. (Genesis 28:10)

   He dreams of a ______________. God promises to be with Jacob. (Genesis 28:12)

3. Jacob goes to live with his mother's family in ______________. (Genesis 29:4)

4. On his way home twenty years later, Jacob wrestles with God at ____________. (Genesis 32:22-32)

5. Jacob reconciles with Esau and settles back in Canaan.

6. Jacob returns to __________ (Genesis 35:1) on God's instructions. There God renews the covenant with Jacob and confirms his new name.

What Would Jacob's Name Be From Now On?

In Genesis 32:27-28, Jacob's name is changed. Look at the pictures below. Choose the picture in each group that does not belong with the other three. Write the letter of that odd picture in the blank space at the end of the row.

Why were names so important in the Bible?

Do you know what your name means?

What would you like it to mean?

Where Do You Go?

Where would you turn if something awful happened to you?

Joseph was in prison in Egypt for something he didn't do. But Joseph survived. How do you think he did it?

Solve the puzzle below to discover some help. Check your answer by reading Psalm 46:1.

Add 6 to each number:

A	B	C	D	E	F	G	H	I	J	K	L	M
25	49	32	62	81	15	89	75	56	10	8	17	91

Subtract 6 from each number:

N	O	P	Q	R	S	T	U	V	W	X	Y	Z
16	23	54	47	78	66	38	96	12	60	88	21	19

95 17 68   62 60   17 90 72

72 87 21 90 95 87   31 10 68

60 32 72 87 10 95 32 81 ,   31   6 87 72 15

48 72 87 60 87 10 32   81 87 23 48

62 10   32 72 17 90 55 23 87 .

THE HEBREW FAMILY TRAVELS

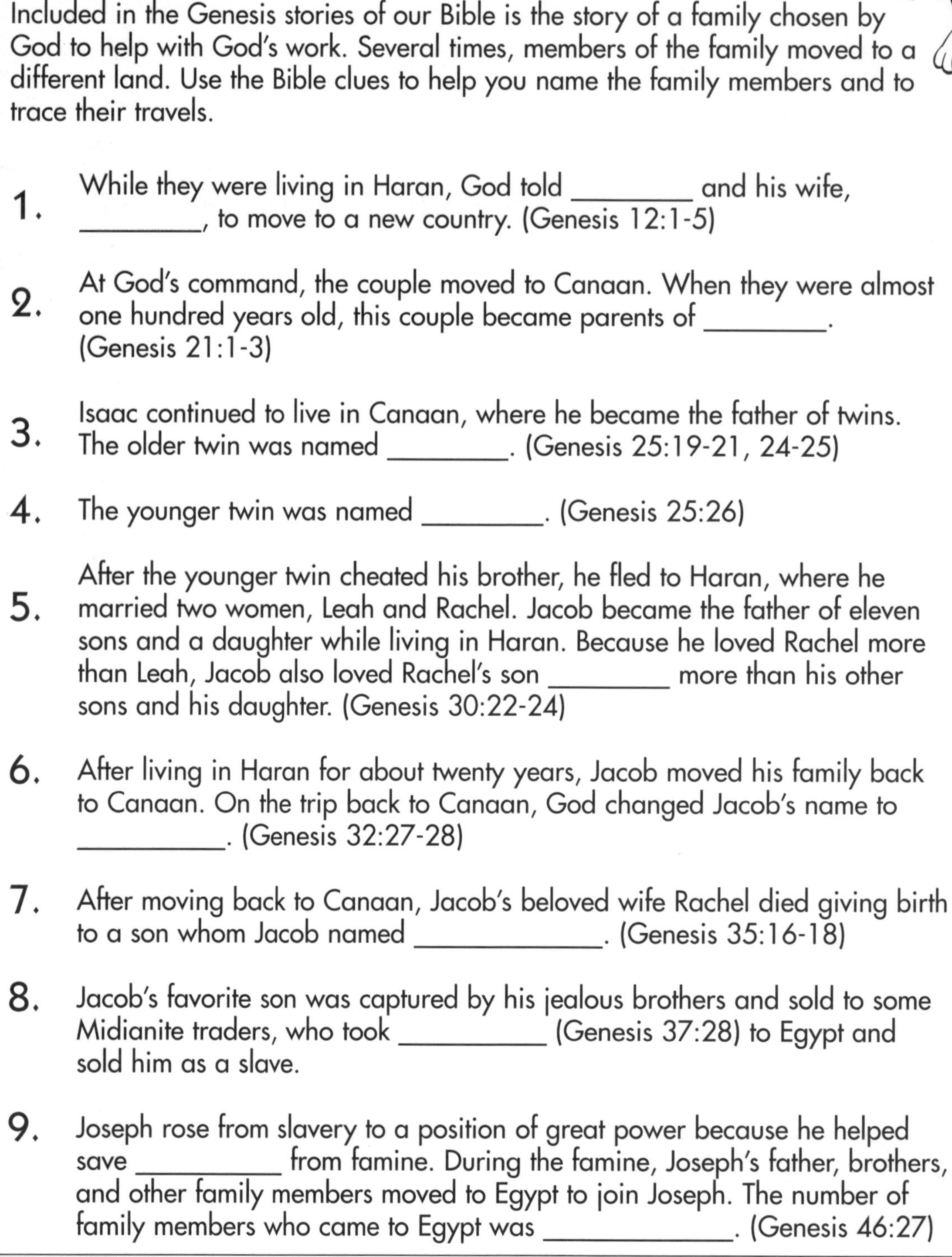

Included in the Genesis stories of our Bible is the story of a family chosen by God to help with God's work. Several times, members of the family moved to a different land. Use the Bible clues to help you name the family members and to trace their travels.

1. While they were living in Haran, God told __________ and his wife, __________, to move to a new country. (Genesis 12:1-5)

2. At God's command, the couple moved to Canaan. When they were almost one hundred years old, this couple became parents of __________. (Genesis 21:1-3)

3. Isaac continued to live in Canaan, where he became the father of twins. The older twin was named __________. (Genesis 25:19-21, 24-25)

4. The younger twin was named __________. (Genesis 25:26)

5. After the younger twin cheated his brother, he fled to Haran, where he married two women, Leah and Rachel. Jacob became the father of eleven sons and a daughter while living in Haran. Because he loved Rachel more than Leah, Jacob also loved Rachel's son __________ more than his other sons and his daughter. (Genesis 30:22-24)

6. After living in Haran for about twenty years, Jacob moved his family back to Canaan. On the trip back to Canaan, God changed Jacob's name to __________. (Genesis 32:27-28)

7. After moving back to Canaan, Jacob's beloved wife Rachel died giving birth to a son whom Jacob named __________. (Genesis 35:16-18)

8. Jacob's favorite son was captured by his jealous brothers and sold to some Midianite traders, who took __________ (Genesis 37:28) to Egypt and sold him as a slave.

9. Joseph rose from slavery to a position of great power because he helped save __________ from famine. During the famine, Joseph's father, brothers, and other family members moved to Egypt to join Joseph. The number of family members who came to Egypt was __________. (Genesis 46:27)

Old Testament Puzzles, © 2005 Abingdon Press

Psalm 139:7—
Hidden Message

Have you ever done anything that was so bad or so embarrassing that you wanted to run away and hide?

Stand back about three feet from this paper and see if you can see the questions asked by the psalmist.

WWWWHHEEERREEECCAAAANNNNIIGGGOOOO

FFRROOMMYYYYOOUUUURRRRRR

SSSPIIIRRIITTT?

OOOORRRRR

WWHHHHHEEERREEEECCCCAAAANNIIIFFFFFLLEEEEEE

FFRROOOMMMMMYYYOOUURRRR

PPPRRESSEEEENNNCCEE?

What Belongs? What Doesn't?

Moses was a very important person. His story has a lot of ups and downs and very interesting twists. What do you know about Moses? Below, mark out every event that did NOT happen to Moses but is part of someone else's story. You will be left with Moses' story in order.

He was born in a stable.

As a baby he was put in the bulrushes by his sister to save his life.

He was raised by an Egyptian princess.

He was visited by three wise men who were following a star.

Out of anger at the mistreatment of a Hebrew slave, he killed an Egyptian.

He stole his brother's birthright.

He fled to Midian after he became afraid his crime was known.

God called to him from a burning bush.

He was taken to Egypt where he helped the pharaoh and was put in charge of all of the grain in the land.

Because he refused to worship any but the true God, he was thrown into a fiery furnace.

He asked the pharaoh to let the Egyptian people go.

After ten plagues were visited on Egypt, the pharaoh allowed him to lead his people out of Egypt.

The Red Sea parted so that he could lead his people out of Egypt.

God gave him the Ten Commandments.

He led the people around the wilderness for forty years.

He led the defeat of the city of Jericho.

He sang to soothe the new king of Israel.

He died before he could enter the Promised Land.

Old Testament Puzzles, © 2005 Abingdon Press

DEBORAH, THE JUDGE

Deborah was a judge of Israel. God used judges such as Deborah to bring justice to people. Deborah was one of the few judges of Israel that not only led the Israelites into battle, but also acted as a judge would act today in the United States—settling disputes among the local people. Deborah was very versatile. We know Deborah was married.

Below, draw lines matching the verbs with the appropriate noun or phrase to discover how we are to live justly with others. To check your answer, read Isaiah 1:17.

Learn to

PLEAD FOR

the widow

the orphan

THE OPPRESSED

seek

justice

defend

do good

rescue

Women in the Bible

Can you name three women who have helped you understand what it means to live as a Christian?

1.
2.
3.

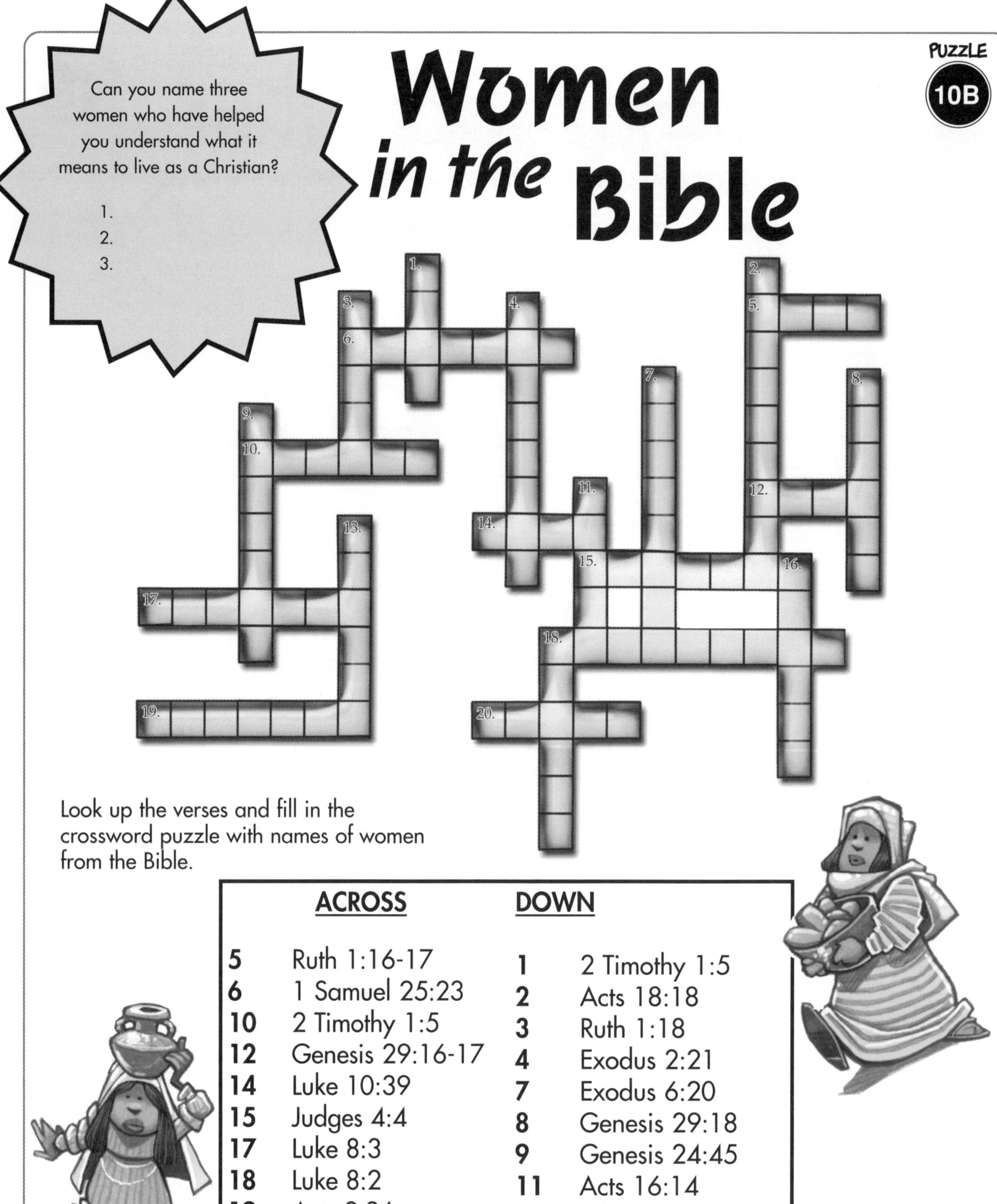

Look up the verses and fill in the crossword puzzle with names of women from the Bible.

ACROSS		**DOWN**	
5	Ruth 1:16-17	**1**	2 Timothy 1:5
6	1 Samuel 25:23	**2**	Acts 18:18
10	2 Timothy 1:5	**3**	Ruth 1:18
12	Genesis 29:16-17	**4**	Exodus 2:21
14	Luke 10:39	**7**	Exodus 6:20
15	Judges 4:4	**8**	Genesis 29:18
17	Luke 8:3	**9**	Genesis 24:45
18	Luke 8:2	**11**	Acts 16:14
19	Acts 9:36	**13**	Luke 8:3
20	Genesis 17:15	**16**	1 Samuel 1:2
		18	Luke 10:38

Important People in Saul's Life

These people all played a part in Saul's life (for good or bad). Use the Scripture to discover who they were.

Played the lyre to soothe Saul.
1 Samuel 16:14-23

____

Anointed Saul king.
1 Samuel 10:1

____

Draw a diagram of some of the important people in your life. What makes them important?

Philistine champion whose height was six cubits and a span.
1 Samuel 17:4

____

Saul's son and a good friend of David's.
1 Samuel 13:16

____

Go Figure!

David used a lyre when playing for Saul and singing psalms.

Solve the math problems below to find the chapter and verse in Psalms that tells how many strings are on a lyre (referred to in some translations as a harp).

Solve each line of the problem. For lines two and three, put the answer from the preceding line in the first blank of the problem.

Problem A: Solve all three lines to find the <u>chapter</u> in the Book of Psalms.

1. 48 ÷ 6 = _______

2. _______ + 3 = _______

3. _______ × 3 = _______

Problem B: Solve all three lines to find the <u>verse number</u> in that chapter.

1. 8 × 9 = _______

2. _______ - 42 = _______

3. _______ ÷ 15 = _______

Read Psalm _______:_______ to find that the lyre (or harp) David would have used has _______ strings.

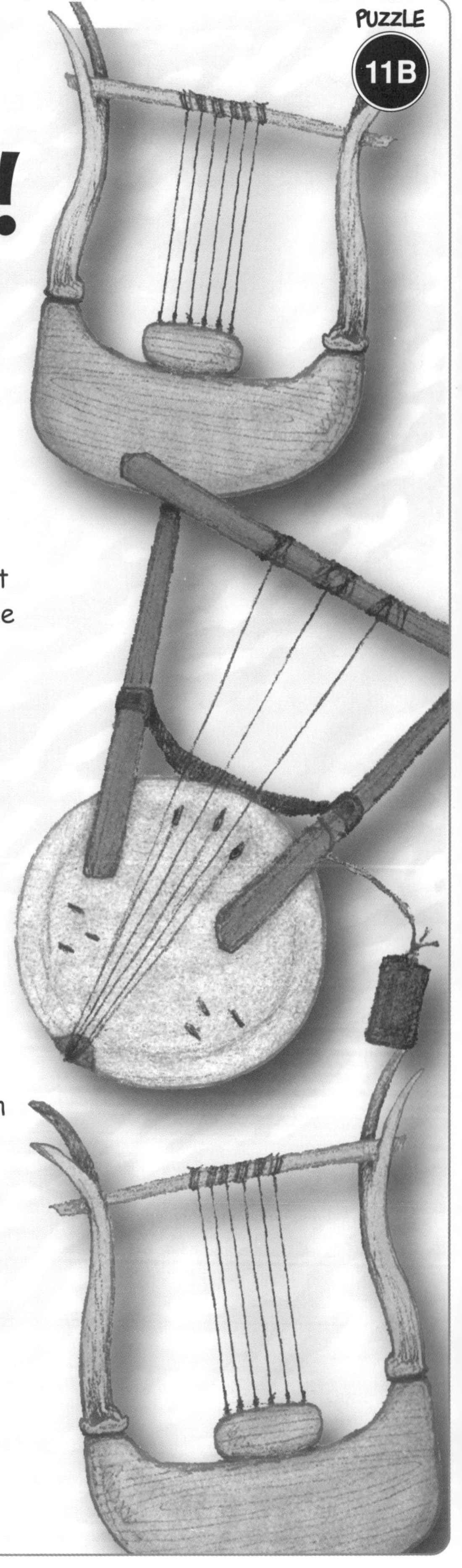

Old Testament Puzzles, © 2005 Abingdon Press

DAVID'S WEB OF SIN

Follow the trail in the maze to discover the scrambled words.
Unscramble the words and use them to complete the sentences.
Use 2 Samuel 11:1–12:15 if you need help.

Hint: The words are in the maze in the order that they go into the sentences.

START

FINISH

If you lied about something really important to your parents, what would the consequence be?

1. David spies _________________ taking a bath.

2. David commits _________________.

3. David sends ____________ to the front of the battle and withdraws protection so that this person would ___________ ____________.

4. David marries _________________.

5. _____________, a prophet, tells David a _____________ pointing out David's sins.

6. David _______________.

7. David is _________________, but still must pay the _________________ for his sins.

Coded Psalm

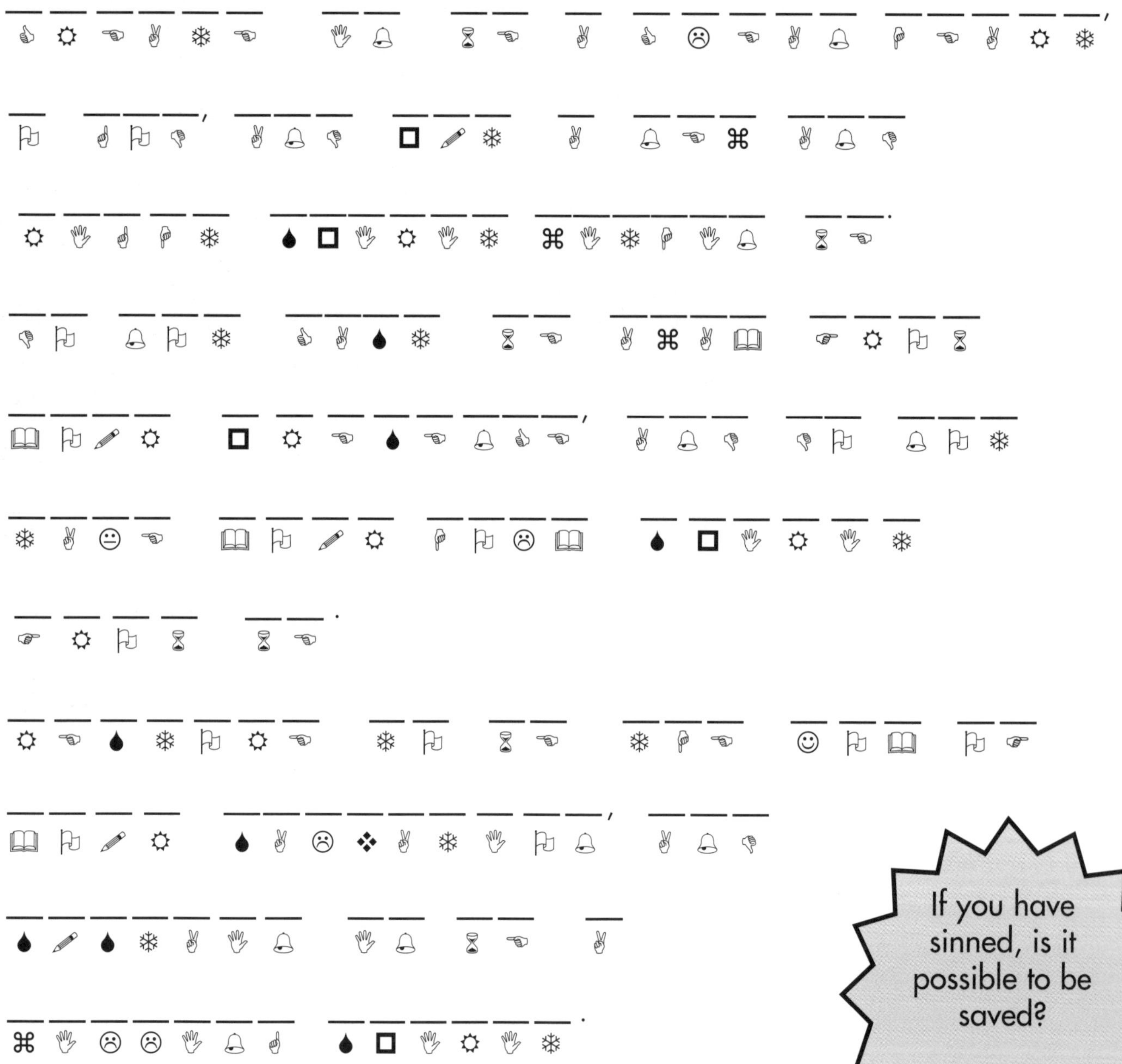

(Psalm 51:10-12)

> If you have sinned, is it possible to be saved?
>
> If so, how?

A	B	C	D	E	F	G	H	I	J	K	L	M	N	O	P	Q	R	S	T	U	V	W	X	Y	Z

Old Testament Puzzles, © 2005 Abingdon Press

Amos's Words About Justice

God gave Amos a message to pass along. However, the words have gotten scattered all over the page. Gather up the words and put them in order on the lines below. Caution: There are words you won't need. You will have to figure out which words to use.

What is your definition of justice? What is an example of a just act?

Hint: Below each blank line is the number of letters that are supposed to be in the word on that line.

LET and
an SING repentance
justice flow down nowhere flop
hope up never river everybody's
REMEMBRANCE MEMORY STREAM
roll around ocean
like GOD believe not
righteousness like MOMENTS
nor ever-flowing waters mine

______ ______ ______ ______
(3) (7) (4) (4)

______ ______, ______
(4) (6) (3)

______ ______ ______
(13) (4) (2)

______ ______. (Amos 5:24)
(11) (6)

From One Beginning to the Next

See if you can put the following events from biblical history in their proper order.

Place a number 1 beside the event you believe begins the story, a 2 beside the second event, and so forth, until you reach 20, the event that promises a new beginning.

a. _______ Esau loses his birthright to Jacob.

b. _______ Saul becomes king of Israel.

c. _______ Judges rule over Israel.

d. _______ The people are scattered for attempting to build the tower of Babel.

e. _______ Moses returns to lead his people out of Egypt.

f. _______ John the Baptist is born.

g. _______ God creates the earth.

h. _______ Jacob and Laban settle their differences by making a covenant.

i. _______ Jesus is born in Bethlehem.

j. _______ Moses kills an Egyptian for beating a slave and runs away.

k. _______ God expels Adam and Eve from the garden of Eden.

l. _______ Joshua leads the Hebrews into the Promised Land.

m. _______ A jealous Cain kills Abel.

n. _______ Abraham and Lot separate and divide the land between them.

o. _______ David of Bethlehem becomes king of Israel.

p. _______ Noah builds the ark in preparation for the Flood.

q. _______ Joseph gets out of prison in Egypt and becomes the overseer of the food of the land.

r. _______ The angel Gabriel is sent by God to Joseph and to Mary.

s. _______ Isaac is born and almost sacrificed.

t. _______ Prophets help the kings of Israel and Judah learn the will of God.

From Advent Through the Judgment of the Nations

SCATTERED → WORDS

Below is a verse from the Bible. Some words have been taken out. Put them back where they belong, arranging them in the blanks until the verse makes sense. The number part of the Bible reference is 30:18. You'll have to discover which book! (Honestly, it will be more fun if you solve it yourself.) How do you do that? Start using your Bible!

To check your answer, ask your teacher for the correct book of the Bible, and look up the verse.

Why do you think we're told to "wait" for God?

Hint: One word is used twice.

Therefore the ___________ ________ to be ______________

to you; therefore he will _________ _____ to show _________

to you. For the __________ is a _________ of ___________;

___________ are all those who _________ for him.

RISE UP

WAITS

mercy

GRACIOUS

blessed

God

wait   Lord   JUSTICE

Quote Fall

The letters in the columns in the puzzle need to "fall" into the empty squares below. Letters in Column 1 can be dropped only into Column 1 of the grid below, letters in Column 2 into Column 2, and so on. A dark shaded box in the grid means that you skip that column and go on to the next column to drop the letter.

HINT: Look at the first "word" in the bottom grid. Since there are three empty boxes, you are looking for a three-letter word. Look at the letters in the three columns directly above these boxes. Which of the letters make a word? Which of the words "fits" or makes sense in the puzzle?

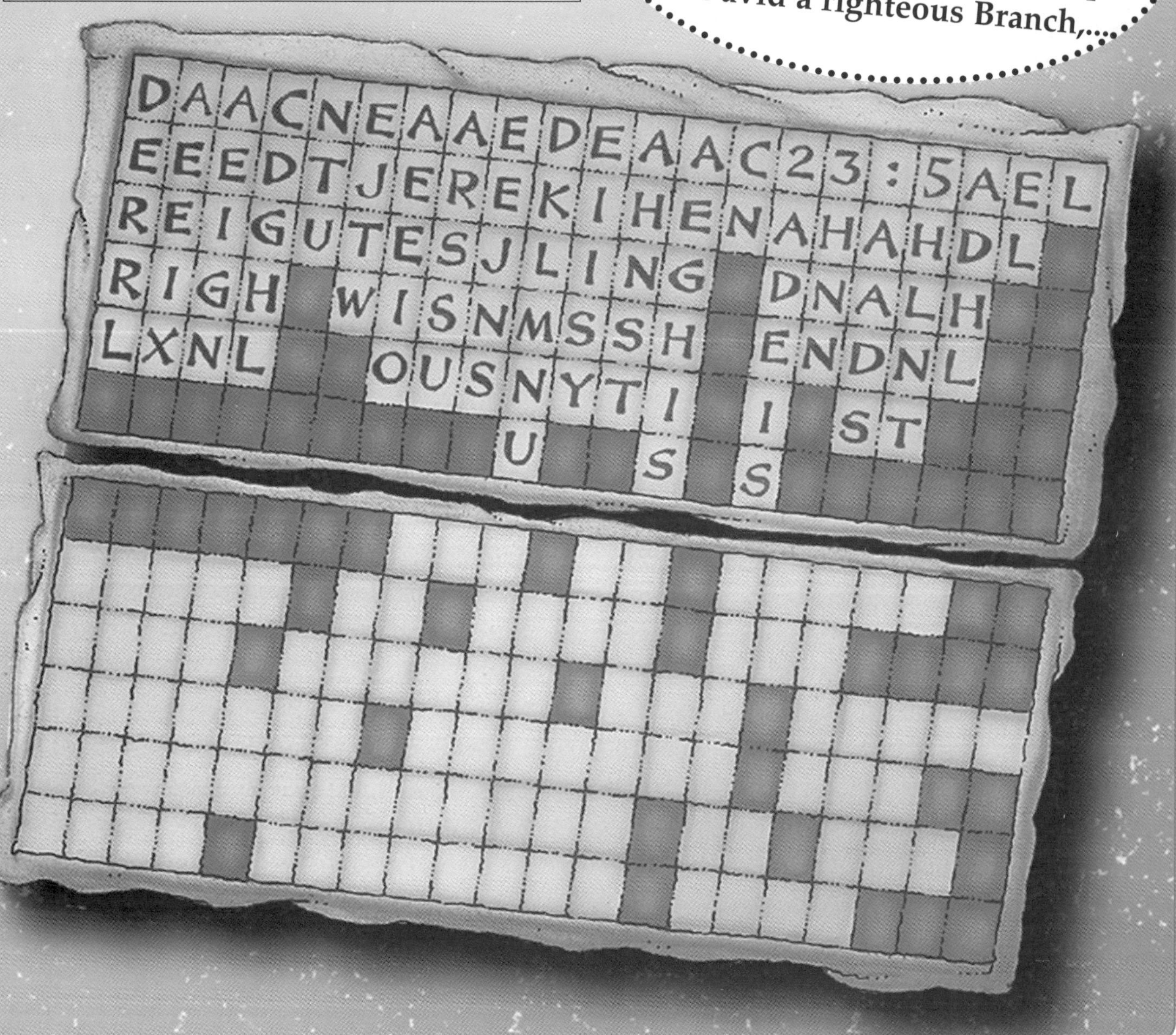

New Testament Puzzles (1), © 2005 Abingdon Press

Color It

Who did the angel come to in a dream in Matthew 1:20-21?
Color the spaces marked with an X to find out. Then color the remaining spaces with other colors.

Do you ever remember your dreams? Have you ever had a dream you felt was really important?

Name Game

Emmanuel means "God is with us." Emmanuel is one of the names we use for Jesus.

Look up these verses. Draw a line to the name for Jesus that you find in the Bible verse reference.

Isaiah 9:6

John 10:11

Matthew 21:9

Matthew 27:37

Matthew 1:23

Luke 1:35

Luke 2:11

Luke 19:39

John 8:12

John 1:36

Savior, Messiah, Lord

IN THOSE DAYS

Have you ever seen your parents fill out a census form? Have they ever mentioned how they feel about being part of a census?

This story is about a census. Fill in the blanks using the words below. Caution: Some words are used more than once.

Read Luke 2:1-7 to see how many you filled in correctly.

In those days a ___________ went out from ___________ ____________ that all the ____________ should be ____________. This was the first ______________ and was taken while ______________ was ______________ of ________________. All went to their own ___________ to be ______________. ______________ also went from the town of ________________ in __________ to ____________, to the __________ ____ ________ called ______________, because he was ______________ from the __________ and ___________ of ______________. He went to be ______________ with _________, to whom he was engaged and who was expecting a child. While they were there, the time came for her to deliver her child. And she __________ ____________ to her ______________ __________ and _______________ him in bands of cloth, and ____________ him in a ________________, because there was _______ ________ ______ _________ ______ ___________ ___________.

Augustus	*family*	*wrapped*	*manger*
birth	*them*	*Nazareth*	*of*
registered	*Galilee*	*house*	*no*
Bethlehem	*firstborn*	*Mary*	*place*
city	*towns*	*in*	*son*
registration	*Joseph*	*Syria*	*gave*
decree	*world*	*inn*	*for*
the	*Judea*	*Quirinius*	*Emperor*
David	*governor*	*laid*	*descended*

CHRISTMAS TIMELINE

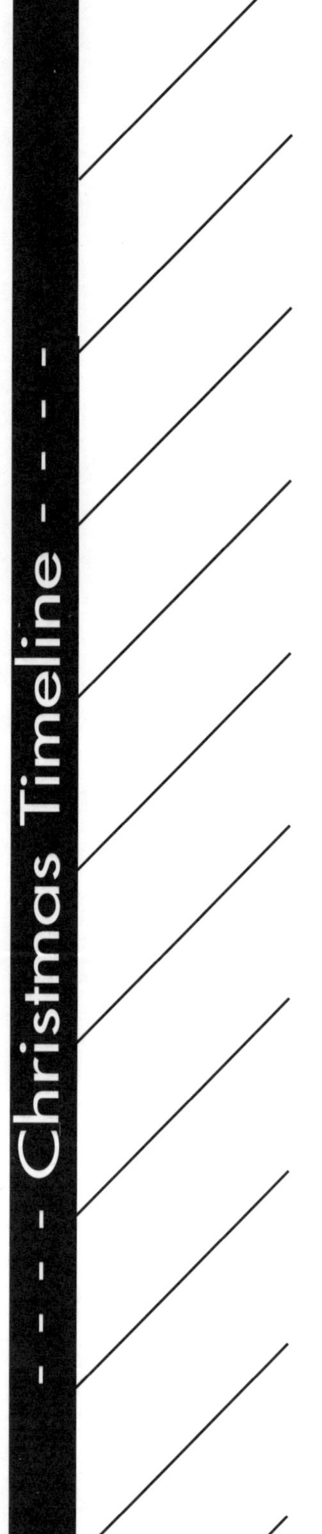

Put the events of Christmas in the correct order on the timeline to the left.

- Augustus Caesar orders the people to go to their hometowns to be registered.

- An angel tells Mary she will have a child.

- Jesus is born.

- Mary and Joseph take the baby Jesus and flee to Egypt.

- An angel visits Joseph in a dream.

- The wise men stop to see King Herod.

- Mary and Joseph go to Bethlehem for the census.

- Shepherds visit Jesus in the stable.

- Herod seeks out the baby Jesus to kill him.

- Simeon and Anna see baby Jesus when he is presented at the Temple.

If you need help, use the first two chapters of the Books of Matthew and Luke.

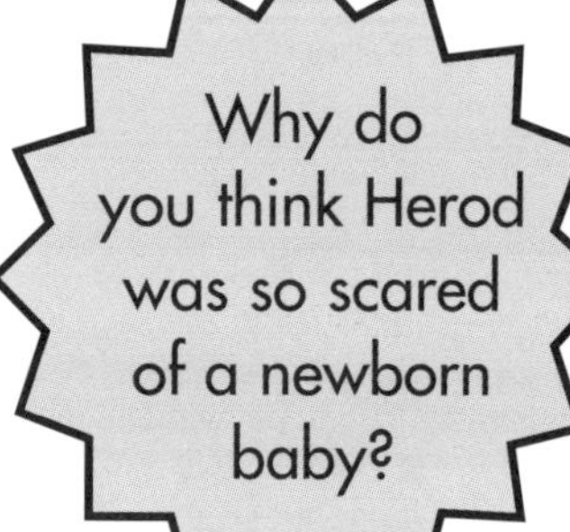

New Testament Puzzles (1), © 2005 Abingdon Press

A Few Crosswords for the Shepherds

All of the answers can be found in Luke 2:8-20.

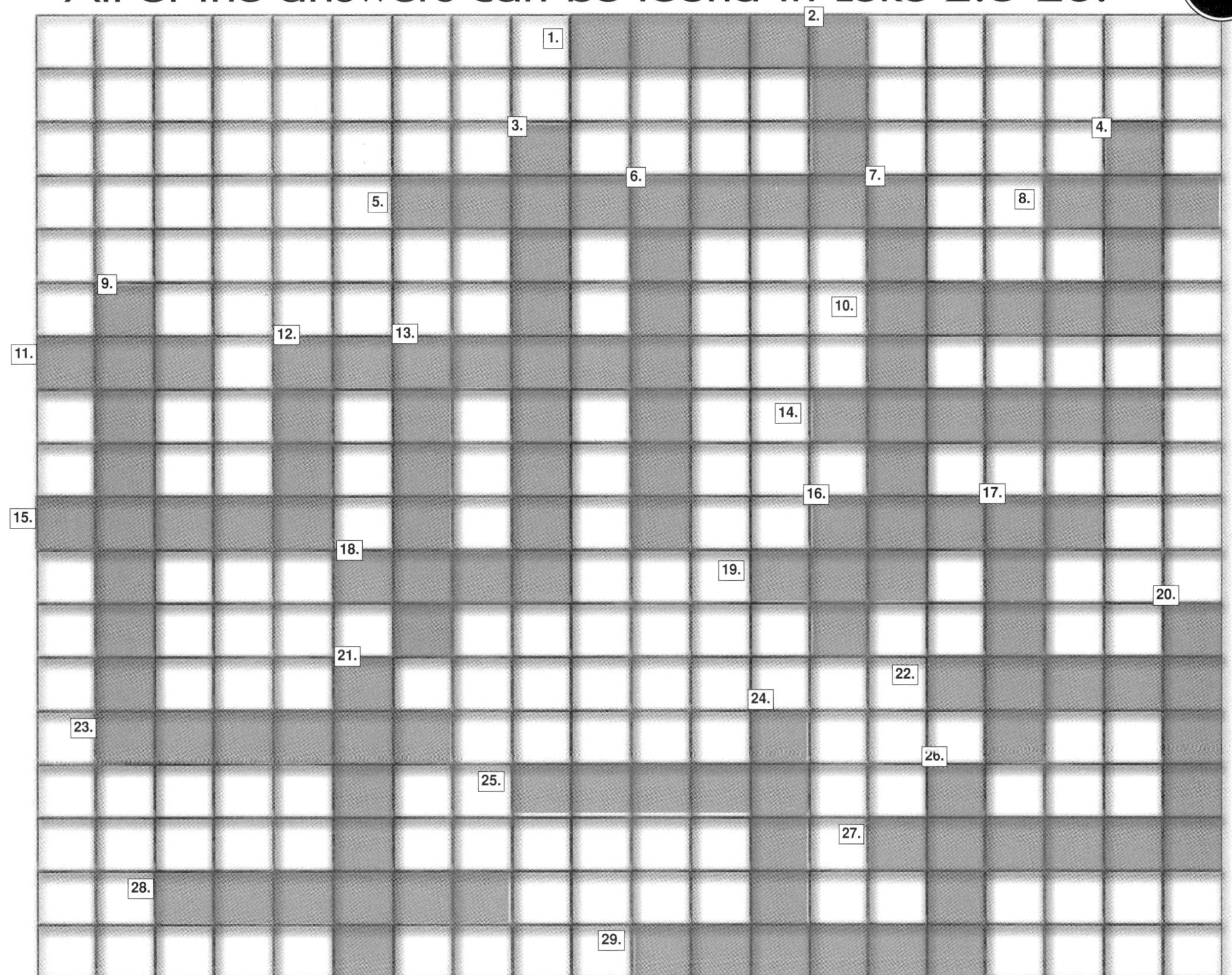

Across

1. messenger
5. sheep tenders
8. object of praise and glory
10. shared Jesus' birthplace
11. 4C—second part
12. Hebrew for Christ
14. large area
15. what the angels gave God
16. bunch of sheep
18. almost the last word
19. happiness
22. wrapper
23. feeding trough
25. makes waste—sometimes
27. all humanity
28. David's descendant
29. shepherd's workplace

Down

2. angel dispatcher
3. totally freaked out
4. when the news isn't bad
6. not the lowest earth
7. unexpectedly
9. city of David
12. female parent
13. rescuer
16. 4C—first part
17. God's gift–wrapped
20. what the glory did
21. how high the glory got
24. God got glory, earth got _____
26. report of current event

Jesus was sent as our Savior. From what kinds of things do we need to be saved?

Shepherd SQUARES

Directions:

Read Luke 2:8-20, then match each question with the Shepherd's Squares panelist who has the correct answer. Write the numbers of the questions in the squares on the panelists' desks.

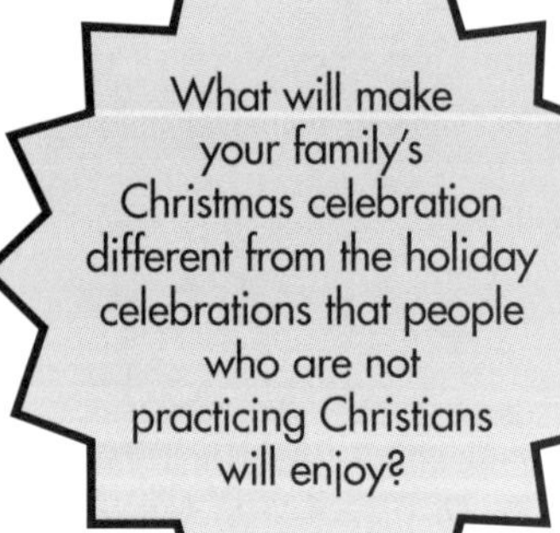

What will make your family's Christmas celebration different from the holiday celebrations that people who are not practicing Christians will enjoy?

City of David panel —

In the fields panel —

Multitude of angels panel —

1. Where were the shepherds watching their flocks?
2. Who said to the shepherds, "I am bringing you good news of great joy for all the people"?
3. Where was a child born this day?
4. What was the "child wrapped in bands of cloth and lying in a manger"?
5. Who said, "Glory to God in the highest heaven"?
6. Who said, "Let us now go to Bethlehem and see this thing that has taken place"?
7. Whom did they find with the baby in the manger?
8. How did people react when they heard the news of the birth of the Messiah?
9. What did the shepherds do as they returned home?

Quickly answer each of the following questions by circling the letter beside the answer that you believe is correct.

1. Which Gospel writer tells the story of special visitors coming to bring gifts to baby Jesus?

    a. Matthew

    b. Mark

    c. Luke

    d. John

2. Which of the following words would not, according to the Bible, describe those visitors?

    a. wise men

    b. magi

    c. kings

    d. astrologers

3. The Bible says there were how many of these visitors?

    a. three

    b. twelve

    c. four

    d. the Bible does not say

4. What was King Herod's emotional state when he became aware that the promised King of the Jews had been born?

    a. delighted

    b. frightened

    c. angry

    d. thankful

5. What did King Herod ask these visitors to do?

    a. take a gift to the baby for him

    b. leave, never to return

    c. return and tell him where the baby was

    d. bring the baby back to him

6. Where did the visitors find Jesus?

    a. wrapped in swaddling clothes and lying in a manger

    b. in a house

    c. in a stable, bedded down in some hay

    d. with Mary on a donkey getting ready to go to Egypt to get away from Herod

7. The visitors knew where Jesus was when the star…

    a. stopped

    b. began to glow brighter

    c. pulsed gently

    d. disappeared

8. Jesus' visitors were warned not to return to Herod by…

    a. a messenger from the priests and scribes

    b. the shepherds

    c. Joseph and Mary

    d. a dream

9. How was Joseph warned to flee with Jesus and Jesus' mother to Egypt?

    a. by the visitors

    b. by his neighbors

    c. by an angel of the Lord in a dream

    d. by two men sent from God

10. How long did Mary and Joseph remain with Jesus in Egypt?

    a. until the death of Herod

    b. until Herod declared an amnesty

    c. until they heard that Herod had stopped looking for the new King

    d. until an angel told them to return

Bonus Question: What was the reason it was necessary for Jesus to go to Egypt?

One to five points: Time to get some of those details in place! Review Matthew 2:1-23.

Six to eight points: There's hope for you yet!

Nine to ten points: You are an Epiphany phenomenon!

More than ten points: We're going to need a recount!

THE SEARCH

The magi and King Herod were both looking for the newborn King. How were their searches similar? How were they different? Read Matthew 2:1-12 to find out.

Use some of these questions to start two lists below. Add anything else you can think of.

Why were they looking for Jesus?
How did they find out where the newborn baby was?
What did they plan to do when they found Jesus?
How long did their searches take?

The Magi's Search

Herod's Search

New Testament Puzzles (1), © 2005 Abingdon Press

Remember These

It is very difficult to resist temptation on our own, but we are not on our own. God has given us guidance through the Bible. We can use the same Scripture that Jesus used for resisting temptation. Scripture can help you through times of temptation (even the one that was not used in the struggle with Satan).

Match the Bible verse with the correct Bible reference.

one does not live by bread alone, but by every word that comes from the mouth of God.

MATTHEW 4:7

Do not put the Lord your God to the test.

MATTHEW 4:4

Away with you, Satan!

MATTHEW 4:10B

Matthew 4:10a

Worship the Lord your God, and serve only him.

Matthew 4:17

Repent, for the kingdom of heaven has come near.

How do you resist temptation?

SACRAMENT

Before Jesus started his ministry, he was baptized. Baptism is a sacrament of the church; it is a very special moment.

Read John 1:32 and Genesis 8:8-9. What animal do you find in both verses? Connect the dots to find it.

The answer to this puzzle is a symbol of baptism. What does it stand for?

Start

end

New Testament Puzzles (1), © 2005 Abingdon Press

Mystery Word Puzzle

Jesus announced his ministry in his hometown synagogue in Nazareth.

Complete the Bible verse (Luke 4:18-19) to find the answers to the acrostic. When you have finished putting the words in the puzzle, read the letters in the square from top to bottom. What is the mystery word?

Clues to the mystery:

The (4) _________ of the Lord is upon me, because he has (6) _________ me to (7) _________ good news to the poor. He has sent me to (1) _________ release to the (2) _________ and (8) _________ of sight to the (3) _________, to let the (5) _________ go free, to proclaim the year of the Lord's favor.

1. _ _ _ _ _ _ _ _
2. _ _ _ _ _ _ _
3. _ _ _ _ _
4. _ _ _ _ _
5. _ _ _ _ _ _ _ _
6. _ _ _ _ _ _
7. _ _ _ _
8. _ _ _ _ _ _ _

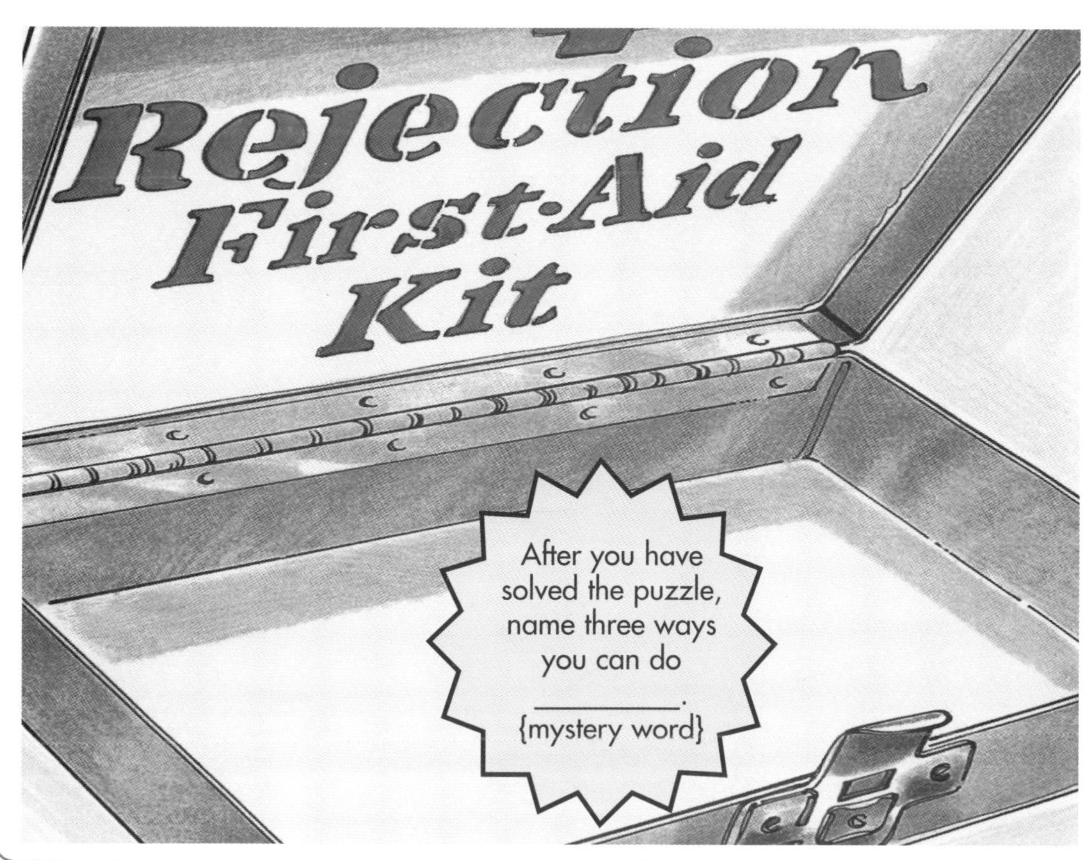

Color-In Puzzle

Color in each space that does not contain one of the words from Luke 4:18:

The Spirit of the Lord is upon me, because he has anointed me to bring good news to the poor.

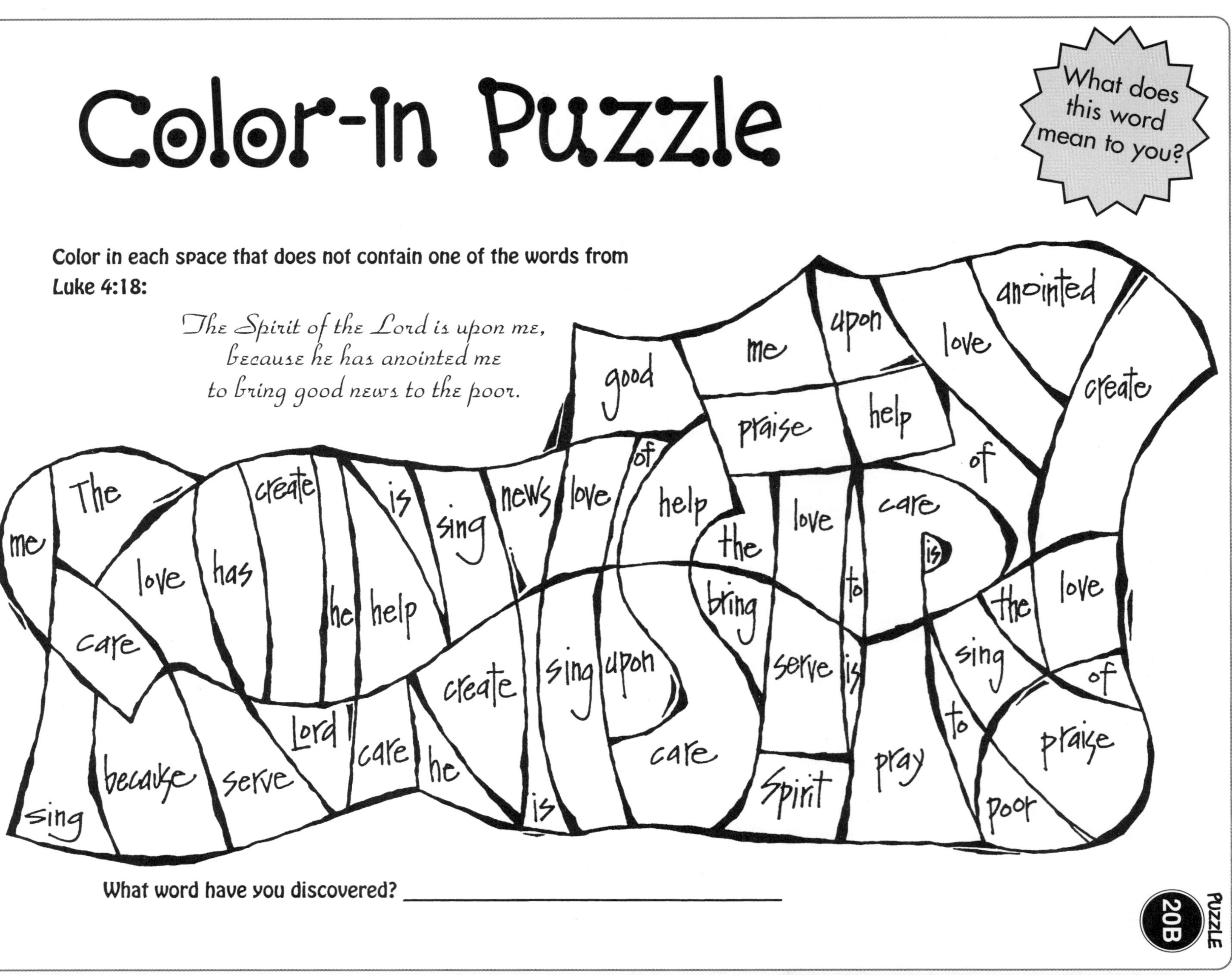

What word have you discovered? ______________________

Cross-Out Puzzle

To work this puzzle, cross out all of the following letters: J K P Q X Z. Going left to right, put the remaining letters on the lines below.

__ __ __ __ ___ __ ____ ______ __

__ __ ____; __ ___ ___ __

_ _____ .

To check your answer, read Luke 10:41-42.

NURTURE Acrostic

How have you nurtured someone in the past week?

Each word in the puzzle is the name of someone in the Bible who nurtured other people. Look up each Scripture reference in the Bible to solve the puzzle.

New Testament Puzzles (1), © 2005 Abingdon Press

Choose

Fill in the blanks in the story by choosing from the possible answers below each blank.
Hint: One of the blanks has three choices that all mean the same thing, and so all three are correct.

Jesus entered ________________________ and was passing through it. A man was
(Jerusalem, Bethany, Jericho)

there named ____________________; he was a chief ________________________ and was rich.
(Barnabas, Zacchaeus, Peter)   (tax collector, priest, tribal leader)

He was trying to see who Jesus was, but on account of the crowd he could not, because he was

____. So he ran ahead and
(too late, Jesus had gone; short in stature; kept away by the disciples)

____________________________ a ____________________________________ to see him,
(climbed, borrowed, ran to the top of)   (sycamore tree, a fast horse, a large tower)

because he was going to pass that way. When Jesus came to the place, he ____________________________
(sat down, looked up, turned around)

and said to him, "____________________________, ____."
(Barnabas, Zacchaeus, Peter)   (go away, I need to talk with you, hurry and come down)

So he did as Jesus said. All who saw it began to ____________________and said, "He has
(sing, grumble, tell jokes)

____ one who is
(gone to be the guest of, been too nice to, gone traveling with)

a ____________________." ____________________________ said to the Lord, "Look, __________ of my
(drunk, foreigner, sinner)   (Barnabas, Zacchaeus, Peter)   (half, all, some)

possessions, Lord, I will ____; and if I have ____________________________
(give to the poor, share with my brother, invest)   (defrauded, cheated, stolen from)

anyone of anything, I will pay back ________________ as much."
(twice, half, four times)

(based on Luke 19:1-9)

To learn Jesus' reply, complete the next puzzle.

How might you influence someone to change his or her bad ways and do better?

WORD Maze

What was it that brought about Zaccaheus's salvation?

Follow the maze and write down the words in the maze to find what Jesus said in Luke 19:9.

New Testament Puzzles (1), © 2005 Abingdon Press

Help Bob, Please!

Bob has agreed to give a short talk on discipleship during worship on Sunday. Bob wants to tell some things about the first disciples and has gotten all confused and can't get his facts straight. Help Bob by looking at the facts logically and sorting through them to help him with his notes. Remember that each pair is known for something different.

There were three pairs of disciples that Bob wanted to talk about. Andrew and Peter were one pair, James and John the second pair, and Paul and Barnabas the third pair. Of these three pairs, two pairs are brothers. One pair (not any relation to each other), Paul and Barnabas, were not part of the original twelve disciples.

Of these three pairs, one pair has a brother who preached a great sermon on Pentecost. One pair traveled to many different countries to spread the good news. Another pair were favorites of Jesus and were with him often when he withdrew from the crowds. They asked Jesus, "Grant us to sit, one at your right hand and one at your left, in your glory" (Mark 10:37). Hint: Read Mark 10:35-37.

Paul was not at the Pentecost celebration.

Andrew had a brother who was a great preacher.

James and John may have done lots of traveling, but they were not noted for it.

Hint: If you need more help, read Acts 2.

______________ was the man who preached the first great sermon on Pentecost.

____________ and ___________ traveled to many places together, including to Antioch.

___________ and __________ asked Jesus to put them in the greatest position.

Use the grid below to help you find the answer. Mark the grid with • for things that are right; mark it with X to eliminate things.

	Brothers	Asked for Great Position	Preached	Traveled
Andrew and Peter				
James and John				
Paul and Barnabas				

To find out what Jesus replied to this last set of disciples, complete the puzzle on the next page.

It's Not Hot

Below we have forgotten to put the spaces between the words. Put slashes between the words below and then take out all of the "hot" words. Place the words you have left on the lines below to discover today's Bible verses.

BUTITISHOTNOTSOAMONGHOTYOUBUTHOTWHOEVERHOTWISHES
HOTTOBECOMEHOTGREATAMONGHOTYOUMUSTBEYOURHOT
SERVANTHOTANDWHOEVERHOTWISHESHOTTOHOTBEHOTFIRST
HOTAMONGYOUHOTMUSTBEHOTSLAVEHOTOFHOTALL.

Check your answer by reading Mark 10:43-44.

____

______ ; ____________________

____

__________________________ ,

____

________________ .

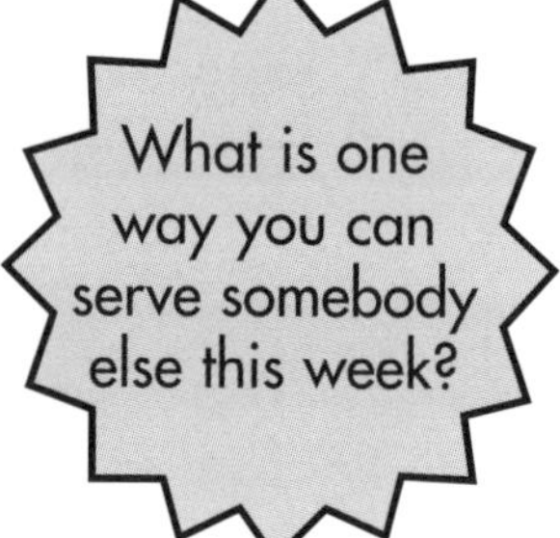

New Testament Puzzles (1), © 2005 Abingdon Press

Letters of Forgiveness

Discover one of the most important things about forgiveness by solving the code.

Hint: G = F
        P = O
        S = R

Check your answer by looking up Matthew 6:14-15.

G P S   J G   Z P V   G P S H J W F

P U I F S T   U I F   J S

U S F T Q B T T F T ,   Z P V S

I F B W F O M Z   G B U I F S

X J M M   B M T P   G P S H J W F   Z P V ;

C V U   J G   Z P V   E P   O P U

G P S H J W F   P U I F S T ,

O F J U I F S   X J M M   Z P V S

G B U I F S   G P S H J W F

Z P V S   U S F T Q B T T F T .

23 % 6 45-89 =0

Numbers, Numbers, and Numbers

In the parable of the unforgiving servant (Matthew 18:23-35), two amounts of money are mentioned: talents and denarii. Can you figure out what each servant might owe today using the formula below?
(Pick an hourly wage to put into the formula.)

Talents—hourly wage **X** 40 **X** 52 **X** 10,000 =
    (what the first slave owed)

Denarii—hourly wage **X** 8 **X** 100 =
    (what the second slave owed)

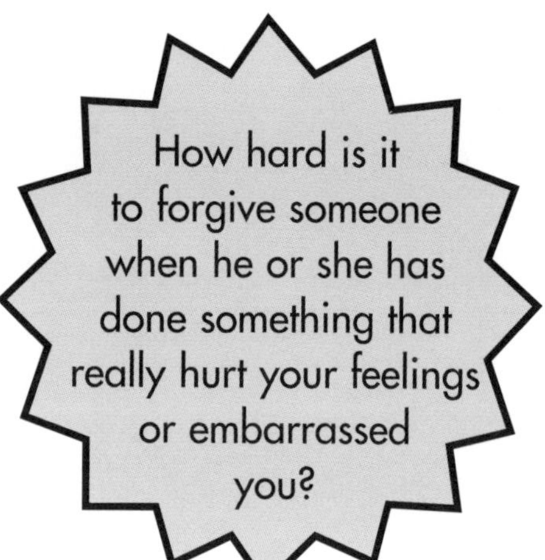

How many times did Jesus tell us we must forgive someone in Matthew 18:22?

Figure it out for yourself.

10 **X** 6 = _________

15 ÷ 3 = _____

6 **X** 2 = ______

Add the three answers to get the number of times Jesus told us to forgive.

New Testament Puzzles (1), © 2005 Abingdon Press

Beatitude Math Puzzle

Write out the alphabet then do the math to figure out the beatitude spelled out below.

___ ___ ___ ___ ___ ___ ___   ___ ___ ___
F-4 K+1 G-2 O+4 T-1 C+2 F-2   H-7 V-4 B+3

___ ___ ___ ___ ___   ___ ___   ___ ___ ___ ___
W-3 K-3 K+4 U-2 A+4   Z-3 J-2   N+1 B-1 Q+1 H-3

___ ___ ___ ___ ___ ___ ___   ___ ___ ___   ___ ___ ___
Q-1 F-1 W-5 R+1 I-4 B+1 V-1   S+1 F-1 B+2   E+1 M+2 N+4

___ ___ ___ ___ ___ ___ ___ ___ ___ ___ ___ ___ ___
S-1 G+2 A+6 E+3 Q+3 J-5 Q-2 T+1 P+3 L+2 G-2 O+4 T-1

___ ___ ___ ___, ___ ___ ___   ___ ___ ___ ___ ___ ___
V-3 D-3 J+1 C+2   H-2 K+4 Z-8   U-1 I-1 B+3 J-1 V-4 U-2

___ ___ ___ ___ ___   ___ ___ ___ ___ ___ ___ ___
H+1 Q+2   Z-6 D+4 A+4   L-1 K-2 M+1 L-5 C+1 P-1 K+2

___ ___ ___ ___ ___ ___ ___ ___.
K+4 D+2   J-2 H-3 C-2 Z-4 I-4 O-1

Read Matthew 5:10 to check your answer.

Jesus' Teachings

Jesus taught us a lot about how to live. For every clue on the left, circle the correct letter in the word on the right. Then copy the circled letters in order on the blanks below.

Circle the letter before "a"	**S a l t**
Circle the letter after "d"	**B e a t i t u d e s**
Circle the letter after "e" (either "e")	**C o n c e r n i n g a n g e r**
Circle the letter after "o"	**C a n ' t s e r v e t w o m a s t e r s**
Circle the second letter in any of the three words	**D o n o t w o r r y**
Circle the letter between two "o"s	**D o n o t j u d g e o t h e r s**
Circle the letter before "i"	**L o v e y o u r e n e m i e s**
Circle the letter after "L"	**T h e L o r d ' s P r a y e r**
Circle the letter after the second "s"	**D o n o t s t o r e u p t r e a s u r e s**
Circle the letter before "R"	**T h e G o l d e n R u l e**
Circle the letter after "h"	**L i g h t**

___ ___ ___ ___ ___ ___ ___   ___ ___ ___ ___ ___

There should be two words between these words. What are they?
Hint: All the teachings above appear in Jesus' teachings that are called by this name (see Matthew 5–7).

Choose one of the teachings on this page. What is one specific thing you can do this week that comes from these teachings?

New Testament Puzzles (1), © 2005 Abingdon Press

Inheriting the Kingdom

Jesus told us those who were to inherit the kingdom were blessed. Use the definition below each blank to discover Jesus' message.

For I was _______________________ and you gave me _______________,
       feeling we get from too little to eat   edible things

I was _______________ and you gave me ___________________________,
   feeling from lack of water   water, or soda, or tea
                        (Hint: three words)

I was a _______________ and you ___________________ me,
   someone you don't know   being hospitable to someone new

I was _______________ and you gave me _______________________,
  not wearing anything   pants, a shirt, a sweater, a coat, shoes

I was _______________ and you _______________________,
   not well   helped someone who was not well
            (Hint: four words)

I was _______________________ and you _______________ me.
  being punished for a crime   went to see
  (Hint: two words)

Check your answers by reading Matthew 25:35-39.

Out of Order

Cut the words on this page apart and put them in order to read today's Bible verse. How quickly can you do it? Check your answer by reading Matthew 25:40b.

least	did	it	my
it	members	as	the
you	to	who	to
these	are	did	you
of	of	family	one
of	me	just	

New Testament Puzzles (1), © 2005 Abingdon Press

From Holy Week Through Imprisonment of Peter

Some of These Words Are Not Like the Others

Why were the money changers and others doing the wrong thing? (Originally they had been allowed to trade in the Temple to help those who had come from afar.)

Three words in each group are related. Select the one that is different in each group, then put them in order on the lines below. The words will give you today's Bible verse (Matthew 21:13b).

1.	them	our	my	their
2.	door	window	cupboard	house
3.	should	would	shall	could
4.	was	be	had	did
5.	called	run	sit	jump
6.	three	one	two	a
7.	girl	house	boy	woman
8.	soon	of	now	later
9.	prayer	laughing	singing	dancing
10.	and	also	too	but
11.	me	I	mine	you
12.	up	are	down	sideways
13.	making	cake	candy	cookies
14.	it	that	those	these
15.	three	one	two	a
16.	Sunday	Monday	den	Tuesday
17.	play	talk	work	of
18.	teachers	doctors	robbers	bank tellers

______ ______ ______ ______

______ ______ ______ ______

______ ; ______ ______ ______

______ ______ ______

______ ______ ______ .

Cleansing of the Temple Maze

Follow Jesus' path as he cleanses the Temple of those who used it as a marketplace instead of a house of worship.

Be careful to be faithful to the Bible story (Matthew 21:12-17). If you follow something that does NOT appear in the story, you will be led astray and end up at a dead end.

If Jesus threw the money changers out of the Temple, does that mean it is never okay to sell anything on the church property?

New Testament Puzzles (2), © 2005 Abingdon Press

Symbols of
Holy Week

Below are several symbols of Lent and the Easter season. Choose from the Scripture references below the one that explains why that symbol is used. Write the correct Scripture reference below the appropriate symbol. Be careful—just for a challenge there are two Scriptures that don't refer to any of the symbols at all.

What do you consider the most important symbol of Lent or Easter? What means the most to you? Why?

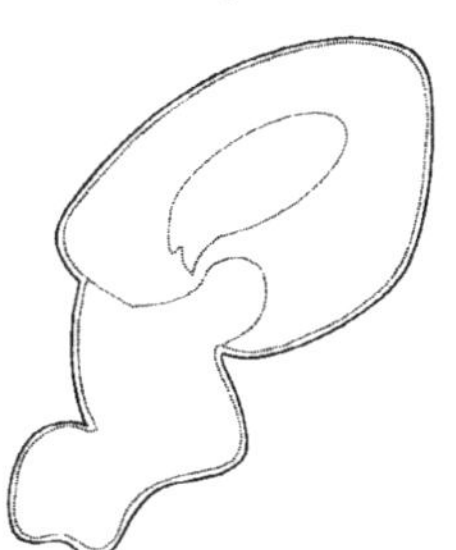

Matthew 26:34   Matthew 27:29   Luke 19:36-38   Luke 22:3-6

John 12:12-13   John 13:5   John 19:38-41   John 20:24-27

Name and/or draw three symbols of the resurrection of Jesus.

What Was the Example That Jesus Set?

Find your way from the words of the verse (John 13:15a) to the letters below. Write down the letters you find. (Hint: Every line does not connect to a letter.) Unscramble the letters and write them on the lines below to answer the question.

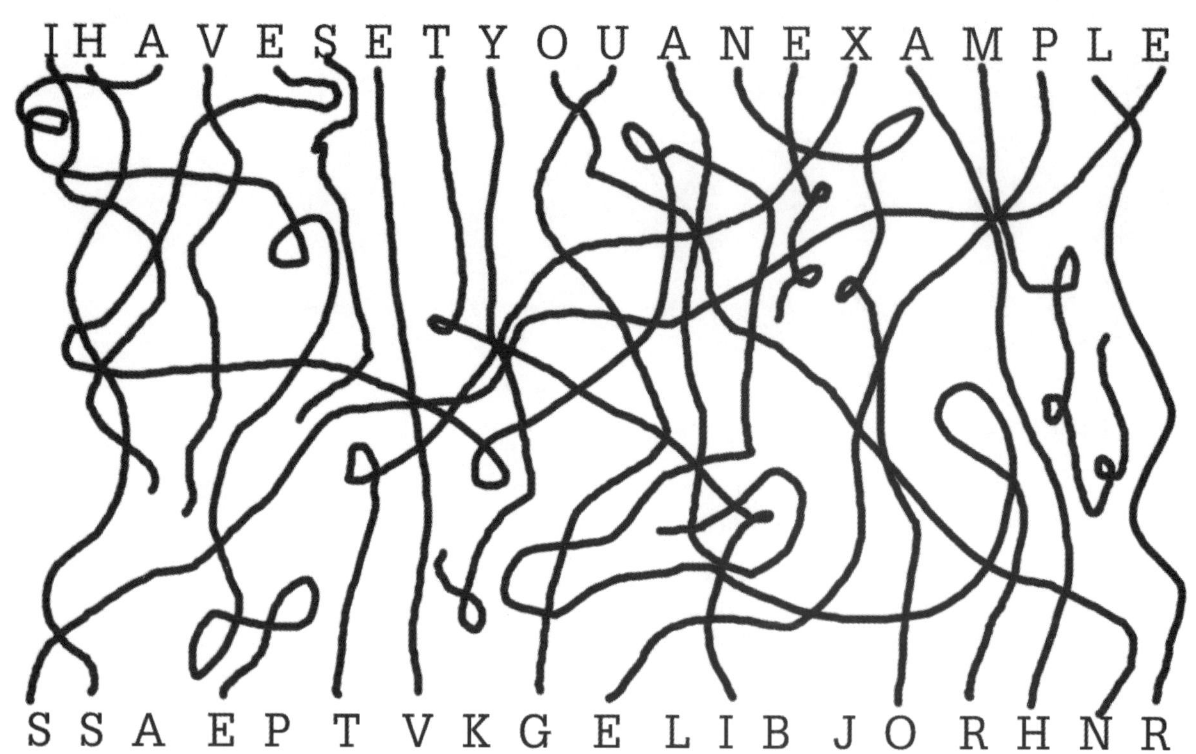

— — — — — — —

— — — — — — —

New Testament Puzzles (2), © 2005 Abingdon Press

Jesus at Prayer

Jesus prayed often. Use your Bible to look up these passages in Luke's Gospel that tell about Jesus at prayer and match them with the description in the other column.

When do you pray? What do you pray for?

His Baptism	**22:41**
During his ministry	**23:46**
Before appointing the disciples	**3:21**
Before feeding the 5,000	**11:1**
On the mountain before the Transfiguration	**9:16**
Before teaching his disciples to pray	**9:28**
Before his arrest	**9:18**
While he was dying	**6:12-13**

WHAT DID JUDAS DO?

After Jesus was condemned, Judas did three things and said one thing. What were they?

Read Matthew 27:3-7.

Judas ____

Judas said ____

Judas ____

Judas ____

What was done with the thirty pieces of silver that Judas had received for betraying Jesus?

____

If Judas didn't want Jesus to be condemned, why do you think he betrayed him in the first place?

Pilate

When Pilate said to Jesus, "Do you refuse to speak to me? Do you not know that I have power to release you, and power to crucify you?" (John 19:10), what was Jesus' response?

Follow the instructions to discover his answer hidden among the words below. Check your work by reading John 19:11.

1. Cross out the fifth word in each line.
2. Cross out all words that begin with the letter "C."
3. Cross out all words with seven letters or more.
4. Cross out all pronouns except "you," "me," and "it."
5. Cross out all words that begin with the letter "S."
5. Cross out any words not found in John 19:11. (There shouldn't be any!)

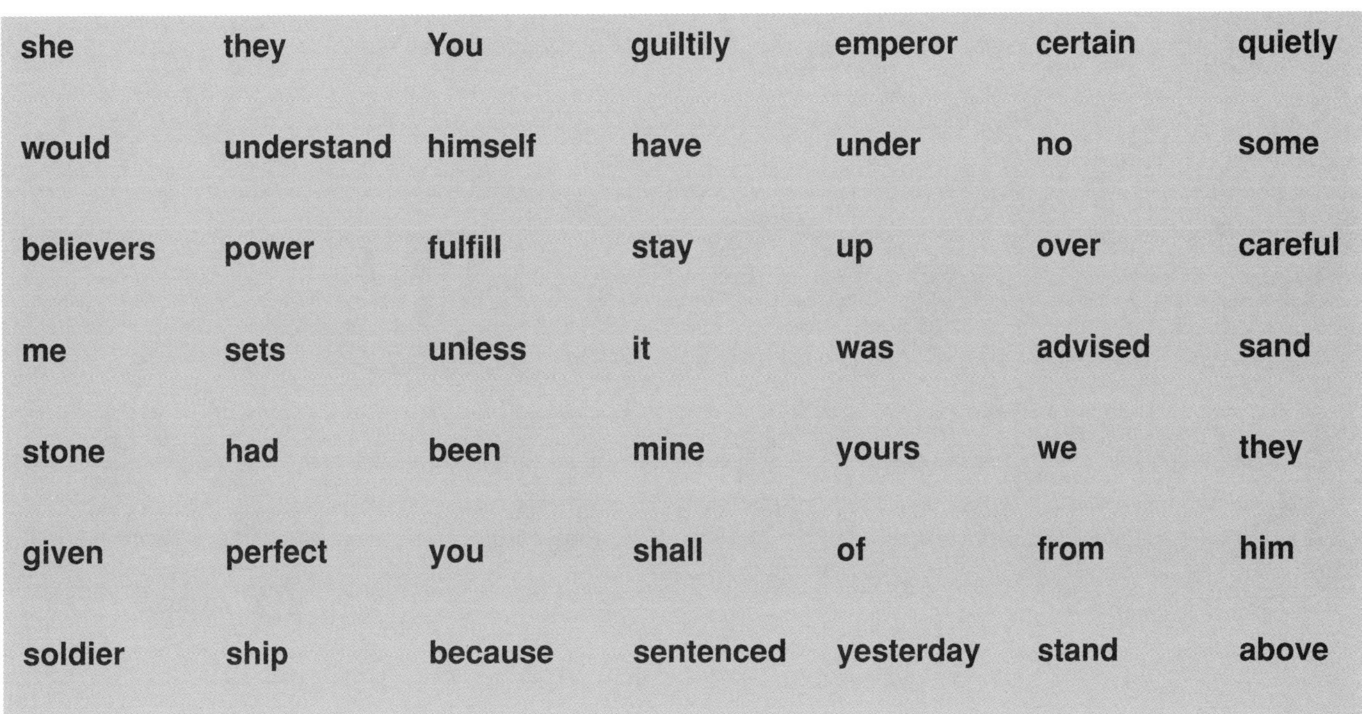

she	they	You	guiltily	emperor	certain	quietly
would	understand	himself	have	under	no	some
believers	power	fulfill	stay	up	over	careful
me	sets	unless	it	was	advised	sand
stone	had	been	mine	yours	we	they
given	perfect	you	shall	of	from	him
soldier	ship	because	sentenced	yesterday	stand	above

GATHER THEM UP

Gather the letters on the page and arrange them in the right order on the blanks to discover something Jesus said to Pilate.

M I T TH
I
o S o y
G L DO R N W
O N m f T
K S D R M

Start here

___ ___. (John 18:36a)

New Testament Puzzles (2), © 2005 Abingdon Press

CHOICES, CHOICES, CHOICES

We all have to make a lot of choices. People in the Bible had to make choices too.

Circle below the choice that was made.

1. Adam and Eve
    a. to say in the garden of Eden.
    b. to eat only those things that God said to eat.
    c. to eat from the tree of life even though forbidden to do so.

2. Abraham
    a. to give Lot the first choice of the land before him.
    b. to choose obedience to God over his firstborn son, Isaac.
    c. both of the above.

3. Jacob
    a. to stay and live as the second son of Isaac and Rebekah for all of his life.
    b. to cheat Esau out of his inheritance.
    c. to give away everything he owned.

4. Joseph of Nazareth
    a. to divorce Mary.
    b. to marry Mary and help her raise God's Son.
    c. neither of the above.

5. The disciples
    a. to leave their normal lives and follow Jesus.
    b. to return home at the death of Jesus and stay there.
    c. to be part-time disciples.

6. Judas
    a. to stay loyal to Jesus.
    b. to turn Jesus over to the authorities in Jerusalem.
    c. neither of the above.

7. The crowd in front of Pilate
    a. to free Jesus.
    b. to free Barabbas.
    c. to free both.
    d. to free neither.

Tried and Sentenced

Do you think Pilate wanted to sentence Jesus to death?

The Bible verses for the events of the trial and conviction of Jesus are listed, but they are not in order. Put the numbers in order below to make a timeline of the arrest and trial of Jesus.

1. Matthew 26:57, 59-68 • Mark 14:53, 55-65 • Luke 22:54, 63-66
2. Luke 23:6-16
3. Matthew 27:1-2 • Mark 15:1 • Luke 23:1
4. Matthew 27:11-14 • Mark 15:2-5 • Luke 23:2-5
5. Matthew 26:47-56 • Mark 14:43-52 • Luke 22:47-53
6. Matthew 27:15-26 • Mark 15:6-15 • Luke 23:17-25

How was Jesus' arrest and trial the same as an arrest and trial today?

How was it different from a trial in the United States today?

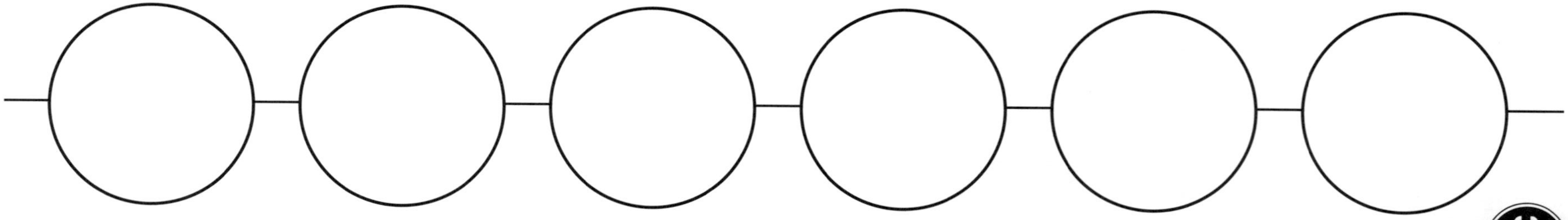

PUZZLE 31B

The Promise

What do we have to do to enter the kingdom of heaven?

Two thieves were crucified with Jesus. Jesus made a promise to one of the thieves. To find out where the thief would be with Jesus, answer the TRUE/FALSE questions below.

For each statement that is true, circle the letter below the T.
For each statement that is false, circle the letter below the F.

Then, write the letters you circled on the lines with the corresponding numbers. If you answered all the questions correctly, you will know where the thief was headed.

1. When Jesus rode into Jerusalem on Palm Sunday on a donkey, this was to fulfill the words of a prophet. (Matthew 21:4)

2. Jesus drove the money changers from the Temple by holding his arm in the air, pointing to the door, and saying, "Out of my Father's house." (John 2:13-16)

3. Jesus washed the feet of the disciples because he wanted them to be grateful to him for what he had done. (John 13:15)

4. Judas betrayed Jesus with a kiss. (Matthew 26:48-50)

5. Pilate was as eager as the high priests to be rid of Jesus. (Luke 23:4)

6. The crowd, when given a choice, asked for Barabbas to be released and called for Jesus to be crucified. (Matthew 27:21-23)

7. Jesus told both thieves who were crucified with him that they would be with him in Paradise. (Luke 23:39-43)

8. After three days they found Jesus' tomb was empty, for he had been raised from the dead! (Matthew 28:1-10)

	T	F
1.	P	O
2.	B	A
3.	S	R
4.	A	Y
5.	C	D
6.	I	O
7.	N	S
8.	E	R

__ __ __ __ __ __ __ __
1. 2. 3. 4. 5. 6. 7. 8.

Who Did _______ Say That I Am? 

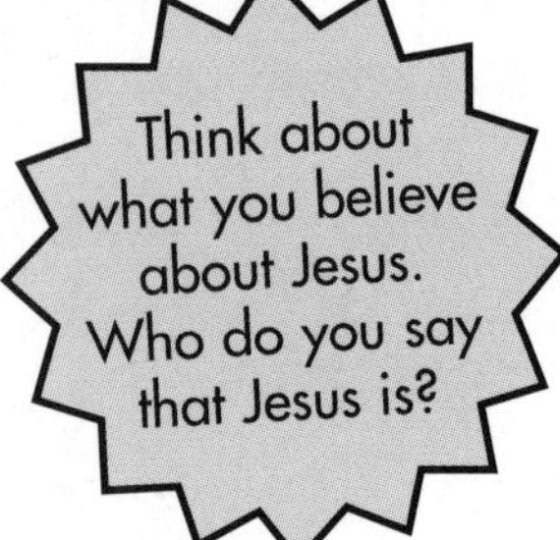

Answer the question, **"Who did_______say that I am?"** for the following people who were involved in the Holy Week story. Write their answer to the question in your own words.

King Herod (Luke 23:11)

Pilate (Luke 23:13-15)

The Roman Centurion (Matthew 27:54)

The soldiers at the foot of the cross (Luke 23:36-37)

Thieves being crucified beside Jesus (Luke 23:39-43)

New Testament Puzzles (2), © 2005 Abingdon Press

EasteR
CROSSWORD

Read Matthew 28:1-10 in your Bible, then complete the crossword puzzle.

1. First name of the two women who went to the tomb.

2. This natural disaster occurred when the women reached the tomb.

3. Who appeared to the women at the tomb?

4. Who did the women meet as they left the tomb?

5. Jesus told the women to tell the disciples to go somewhere. Where was it?

6. What did Jesus say to the women as he met them?

7. An emotion the women had as they left the tomb.

8. The people who shook with fear when they saw the angel.

9. The women did this when they saw Jesus.

10. The angel told the women not to be

_______.

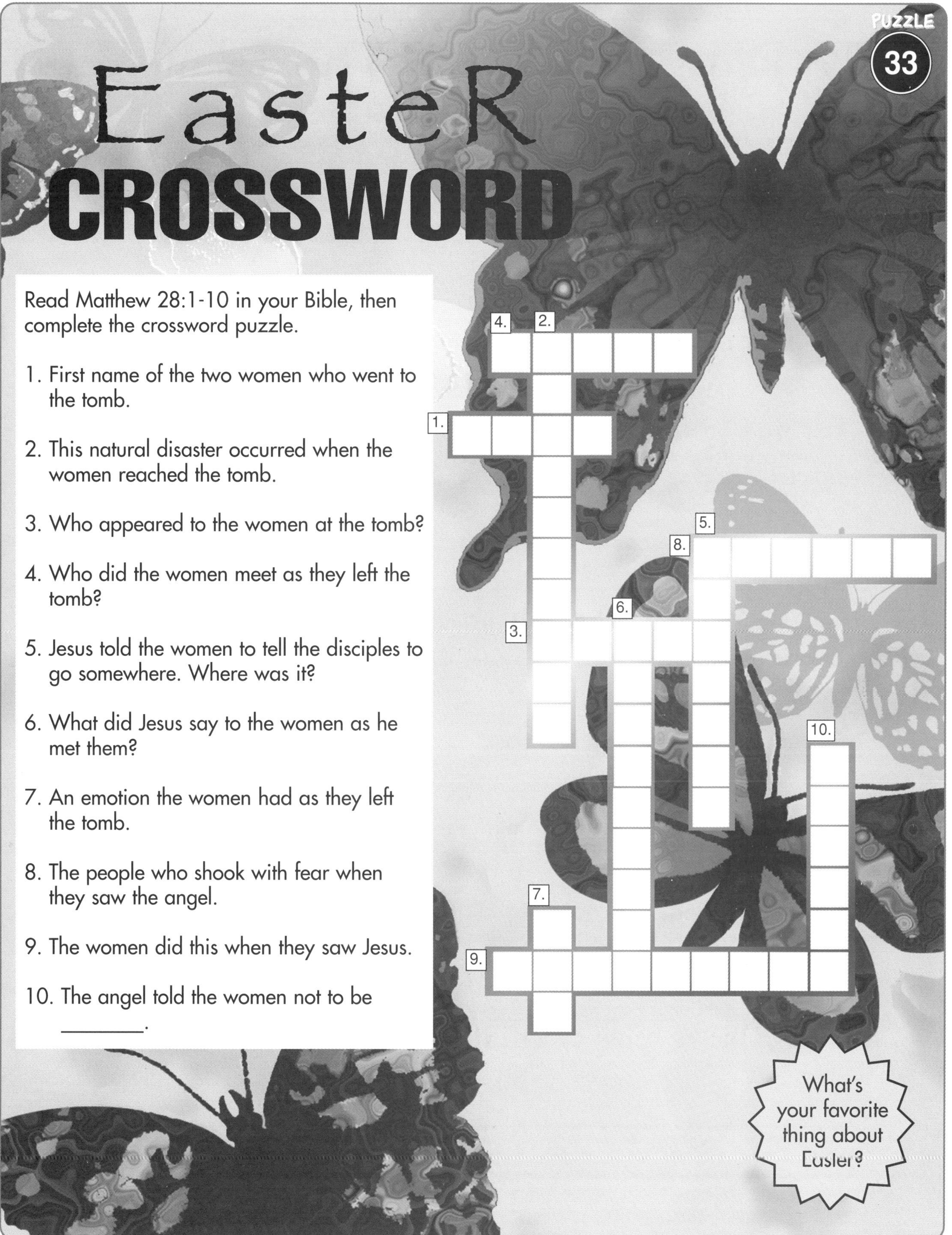

Scripture Logic

Use your powers of logic to figure out what the women were told by an angel when they arrived at the tomb on the first Easter morning to find Jesus missing. Where is Jesus?

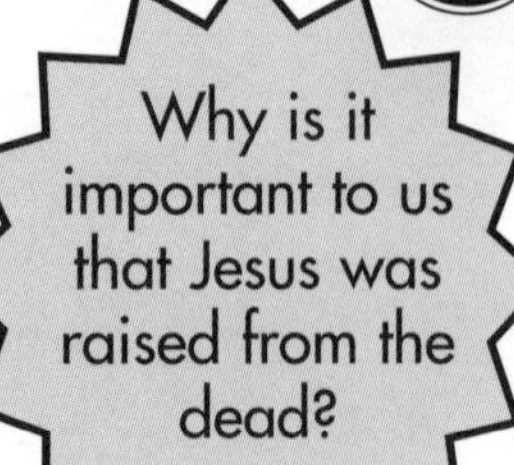

Hint: Write out the alphabet and mark off letters that are not used.

1. Only twelve different letters of the alphabet are used in the twenty-nine total letters that make up these nine words of Scripture.

2. Four vowels are used (these make up thirteen of the twenty-nine letters). One vowel is used seven times. (It is the most popular vowel.)

3. Eight different consonants are used (B, D, F, H, N, R, S and T).

4. Words 1, 4, 6, and 7 all begin with the letter H. The letter H is not used anywhere else.

5. R is used three times. The first time is in word 4.

6. There are two pronouns. They both refer to Jesus.

7. Read the sentences and questions on this page. What kinds of words might be used in this verse?

__ __ __   __ __ __ __   __ __ __   __ __ __ __ ;

__ __ __ __   __ __ __ __ __ __ __ __

__ __ __ __ __ __ __ . (Matthew 28:6a)

New Testament Puzzles (2), © 2005 Abingdon Press

REPORT OF THE GUARD

Look up the following Bible verses, which are found in the New Testament, and gather the words you need.

After you complete that part of the puzzle, transfer the words to the matching number spaces below to find what John 8:32 tells us.

What do you think this verse means?

Matthew 9	eighteenth word in verse 28	1. _____________
Mark 5	eleventh word in verse 28	9. _____________
Luke 3	second word in verse 1	7. _____________
John 14	third word in verse 7	3. _____________
Acts 26	last word in verse 25	8. _____________
Romans 6	tenth word in verse 23	12. _____________
1 Corinthians 1	twelfth word in verse 1	2. _____________
2 Corinthians 1	eighth word in verse 1	4. _____________
Galatians 6	fifth word in verse 2	6. _____________
Ephesians 4	fourth word in verse 15	5. _____________
Philippians 2	first word in verse 2	10. _____________
Colossians 1	fifteenth word in verse 2	11. _____________

| 1 | 2 | 3 | 4 | 5 | 6 |

| 7 | 8 | 9 | 10 | 11 | 12 |

Fill It In

The last conversation Jesus had with Peter before Jesus' Ascension was about what should be done here on earth.

Choose the words from the box on the left side of the paper to fill in the appropriate blanks. Be careful—some words are used more than once, and some may not be used at all! Better read John 21:15-17 to check your answers.

What kinds of things do you think Jesus meant that Peter was to do?

Word box:

love
care
Lord
sing
they
Andrew
these
donkeys
sheep
help
breakfast
like
you
James
Jesus
shout
second
finished
third
lambs
time
Simon
before
fourteenth
tomorrow
again
tend
first
hurt
feed
ducks
everything
Judas
believe
cattle
John

When __________ had __________ __________ , __________ said to __________ Peter, "__________ son of __________ , do you __________ me more than __________?" He said to him, "Yes, __________; you know that I __________ __________." Jesus said to him, "__________ my __________." A __________ __________ he said to him, "__________ son of __________, do you __________ me?" He said to him, "Yes, __________; you know that I __________ __________." Jesus said to him, "__________ my __________." He said to him the __________ __________ __________, "__________ son of __________, do you __________ me?" … And he said to him, "__________, you know __________; you know that I __________ you." Jesus said to him, "__________ my __________."

New Testament Puzzles (2), © 2005 Abingdon Press

STRAIGHT & Curvy

Add a straight line or a curved line to the lines across these pages to discover the day the Holy Spirit descended on the disciples.

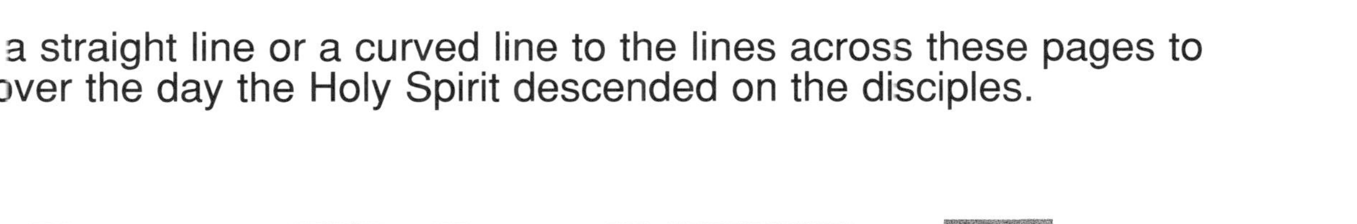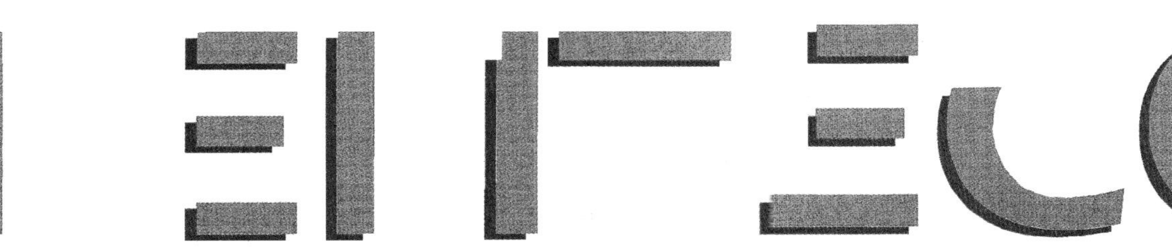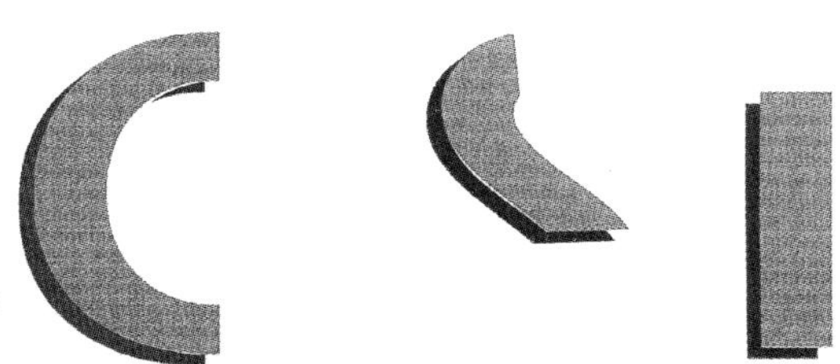

Peter was not known for being a good speaker. Why do you think Peter was chosen to preach on this important day?

It was said that everyone understood in his or her native language. Where did these people come from? (Look at Acts 2:7-11.)

How many different languages can you name?

Hidden Pentecost Message

Choose three different colors. Color in the puzzle, using a different color for each number.

How many men are wearing the number 7?

a = ♥
b = ❖
c = ✖
d = ◆
e = ○
f = ☆
g = ▲
h = ▼
i = ►
j = ☞
k = ✪
l = ★
m = ◗
n = ✉
o = ✎
p = ☎
q = ✂
r = ↕
s = ➜
t = ✿
u = ✚
v = ✍
w = ✈
x = ▢
y = ♣
z = ✿

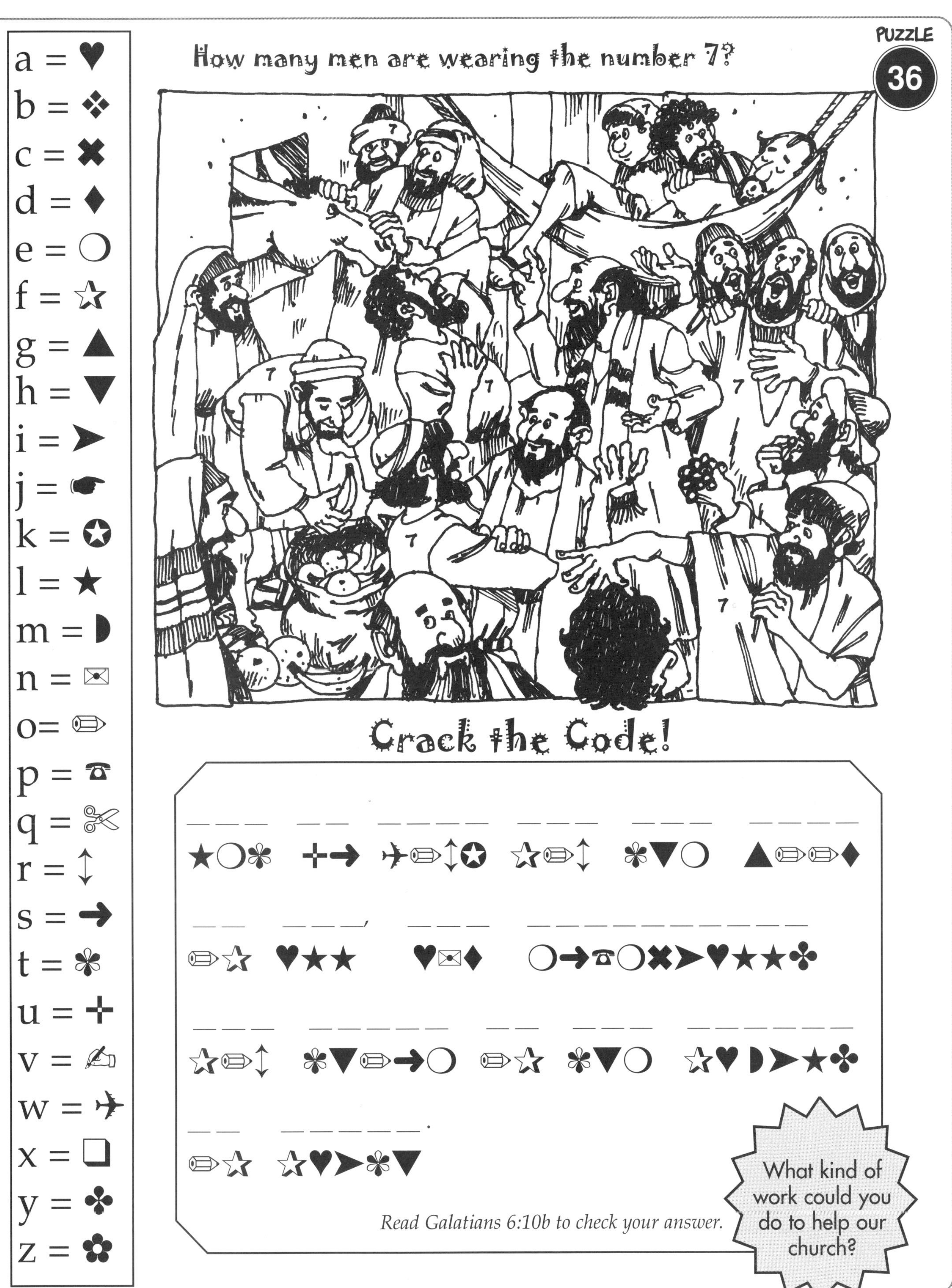

Crack the Code!

Read Galatians 6:10b to check your answer.

What kind of work could you do to help our church?

An Important Number

When the apostles became so busy they could not preach the gospel and take care of all of the faithful at the same time, they chose seven people to take care of the needs of the congregation. Why seven? Why not six or eight? Seven is a very important number in the Bible. Put the words on the bottom of the page in the correct blanks in the puzzle. Check your answers by looking up the Scripture references. Be careful! Some words are used more than once.

Seven is still considered a lucky number, and there are seven days in a week. Why do you think the number seven might be so important?

On the seventh day of Creation, God ___________. (Genesis 2:3)

Jacob worked seven years in order to marry ___________, but he was tricked into marrying ___________ instead and had to work another seven years to marry ___________. (Genesis 29:15-30)

In Egypt Joseph interpreted Pharaoh's dream about seven ___________ and seven ___________ ___________ ___________. Joseph said the meaning was that there would be seven years of ___________ and then seven years of ___________. (Genesis 41:25-30)

When Joshua and his army defeated Jericho, they did so this way: for six days, seven ___________ with seven ___________ marched around the city. On the seventh day the seven ___________ blew trumpets. When they blew a long blast on the ram's horn, a great shout went up and the walls of Jericho fell down flat. (Joshua 6:3-11)

When Peter asked Jesus, "How often should I forgive?" Jesus answered, "Not seven times, but, . . . ___________ times." (Matthew 18:21-22)

John wrote the Revelation to John to seven ___________ in ___________. (Revelation 1:4)

rested   ears of   trumpets   RACHEL   grain   PRIESTS   LEAH   COWS   PLENTY   famine   seventy-seven   Rachel   churches   Asia   priests

It's in the Math

A=1, B=2, C=3, D=4, E=5, F=6, G=7, H=8, I=9, J=10, K=11, L=12, M=13, N=14, O=15, P=16, Q=17, R=18, S=19, T=20, U=21, V=22, W=23, X=24, Y=25, Z=26

Do the math to discover what Stephen did as he was being stoned.

1. Multiply H by B to get ________.

2. Add D plus N to get ________.

3. Subtract Y from Z to get ______.

4. Add K plus N to get ________.

5. Divide T by D to get ________.

6. Add A plus C to get ________.

Now crack the code to see what Stephen asked of God just before he died.

___ ___ ___ ___ , ___ ___   ___ ___ ___
12 15 18 4   4   15   14 15 20

___ ___ ___ ___   ___ ___ ___ ___   ___ ___ ___
8   15 12 4   20 8 9 19   19 9   14

___ ___ ___ ___ ___ ___ ___   ___ ___ ___ ___ .
1   7   1   9 14 19 20   20 8   5   13

Check your answer by reading Acts 7:60b.

Name Maze

In Acts 11:26 disciples were called by a new name. Color the path that completes each maze from beginning to end. When you've finished, write down the letters you find in each maze, unscramble the word, and write the new name on the lines below.

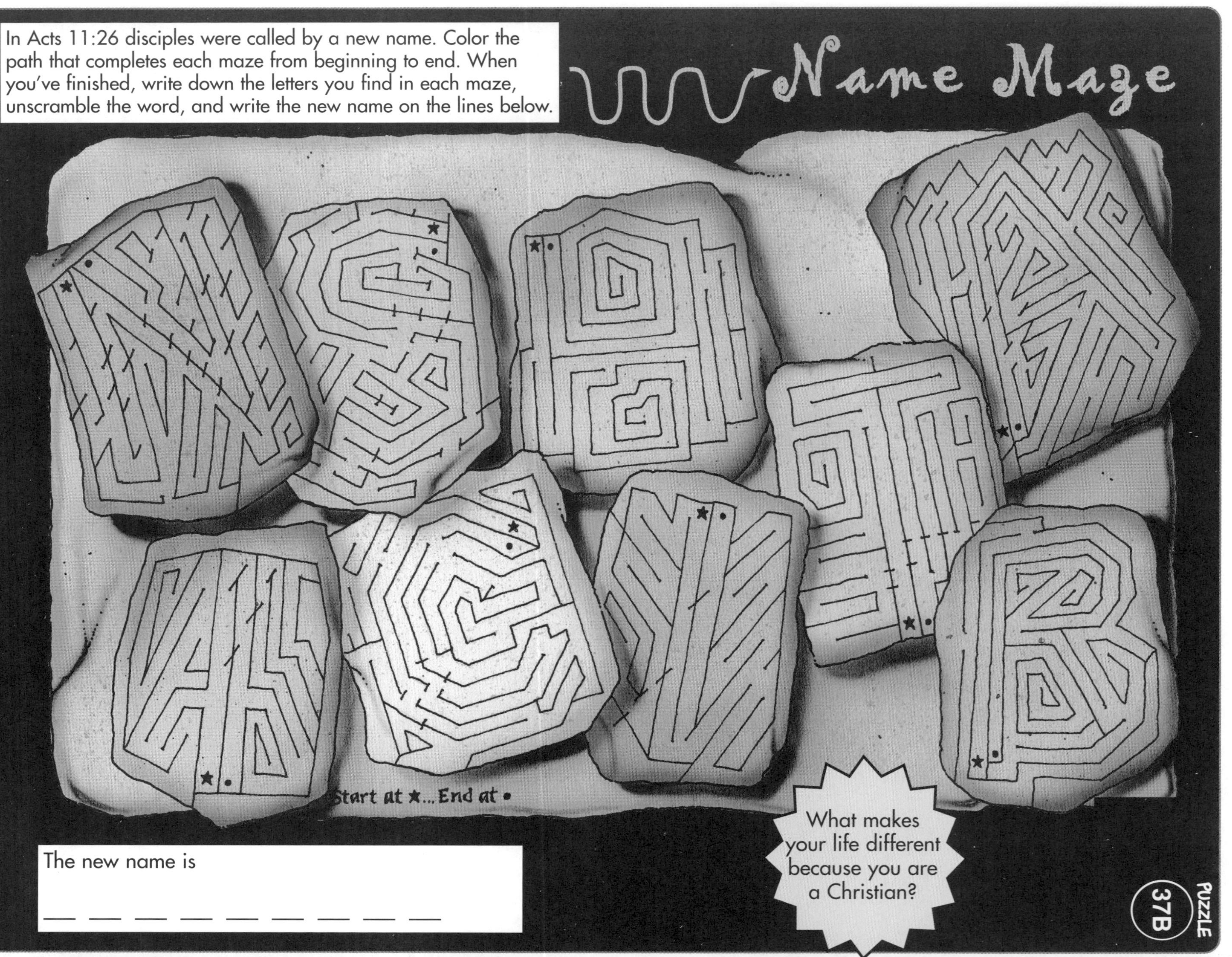

Visit Damascus Road

Unscramble the words below to learn more about a very important man in the early church, Saul/Paul. Check your answers by looking them up in Acts 9:1-20.

1. What was Saul breathing against the disciples?

S H A T T E R and D R U M E R ______________ and ______________

2. Who gave Saul a letter granting him permission to arrest disciples?

G H I H   T R I P E S _______ _________

3. Those arrested would be brought to what city?

E J E L M U S A R ____________________

4. Saul saw a light from heaven as he approached what city?

S U M A C S A D ____________________

5. A voice asked Saul, "Why do you _____me?"

S U E T C R E P E ________________

6. Healing came to Saul at the touch of a disciple. What was the disciple's name?

N A S I A N A ________________

7. What was the name of the street where Saul was healed?

S T A R T H I G ___________________

8. With what was Saul filled?

Y L O H   T I P I R S _________ _________

9. What fell from Saul's eyes?

C L A S S E __________

10. Where did Saul proclaim Jesus as the Son of God?

G Y N O G A U S E ____________________

CROSSWORD

Check the Book of Acts to find the clues you need to complete the crossword.

One person whose life was changed by Jesus was a **13 Across** *(Acts 21:39)* from **17 Down** *(21:39)*. His name in the **4 Across** *(21:37)* language was **3 Down** *(21:37)* and in the **8 Across** *(22:2)* language was **12 Down** *(22:7)*.

He had been brought up to carefully follow the **7 Down** *(22:3)* of his ancestors and had studied under a teacher named **6 Across** *(22:3)*.

A few years after the resurrection of Jesus, this man was working hard to stop the spread of the belief that Jesus was the Messiah.

Breathing **2 Down** and **15 Across** *(9:1)* against the disciples, he had letters in hand giving him permission to go to **10 Across** *(9:2)* to arrest followers belonging to the **9 Down** *(9:2)*, which is what Christians were called, and to bring them back to **13 Down** *(9:2)* in order to stand trial.

On the road to Damascus, he saw a great **21 Across** *(22:6)* from heaven.

He heard a voice saying, "I am **24, 25,** and **26 Across** *(22:8)* whom you are **18 Across** *(22:8)*." Blinded, he was led by his companions into Damascus, where he stayed at a home on **16 Across** *(9:11)* Street.

A disciple named **11 Down** *(9:10)* had a **14 Down** *(9:10)* in which the Lord told him to look for Saul. The disciple hesitated because he had heard how much **5 Across** *(9:13)* Saul had done.

But the Lord told the disciple that Saul would bring the name of the Lord before non-Jews or **23 Across** *(9:15)* and before **22 Down** *(9:15)*.

The disciple found Saul, laid his hands on him, and told him that he had been sent by Jesus so that Saul might regain his sight and be filled with the **19** and **20 Across** *(9:17)*.

His sight restored, Saul was **1 Down** *(9:18)*. The resurrected Jesus had raised Saul to new life, and the story went on!

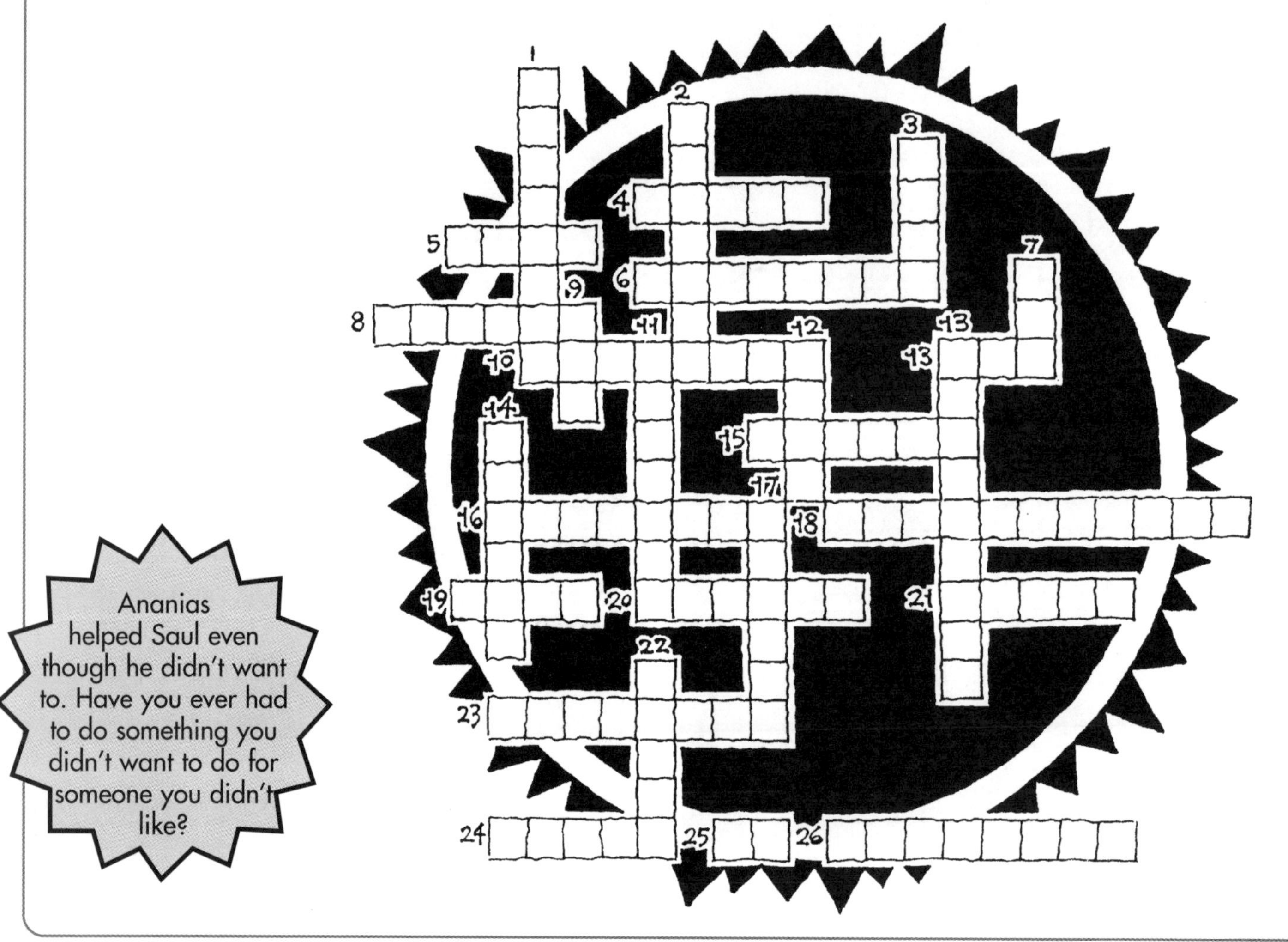

Ananias helped Saul even though he didn't want to. Have you ever had to do something you didn't want to do for someone you didn't like?

New Testament Puzzles (2), © 2005 Abingdon Press

FOLLOW THE MAZE

to find out about what happened to Peter. If you follow the maze correctly, the pictures will tell you the story in the correct order.

If you need help, read Acts 12:5-17.

Who do you think was the most interesting character in this story and why?

BIBLE STORY CHARACTERS

Acts 12:1-19 is much like a movie. And, like in a complicated story, there are several characters.

Beside each character, list what role he or she played in the story.

Herod ____

Peter ____

soldiers ____

guards ____

an angel ____

Mary ____

Rhoda ____

the many who gathered ____

New Testament Puzzles (2), © 2005 Abingdon Press

Puzzles for

SSS

Summer Sunday School

Some Prophets and Old and New Testament Stories of Justice

You can incorporate the puzzles in this section into an overall Bible overview—one that does not use the church year and lasts for twelve full months—instead of using them simply as a summer supplement. Refer to the Scripture Index on page 142. Each puzzle is listed there in order; the puzzles in this section are inserted in the index where their Scripture references appear in the Bible

A BOOK DISCOVERED

During the reign of a young king, the Book of Law was found (it had been lost). Unscramble the words below to discover important information about the story of this discovery. When you have unscrambled all the words, place those letters that are in a circle on the lines below to discover the name of the prophet who helped this young king.

The young king's name was IHJAOS. ___ ___ ___ ___ ___ (___)

The king made a covenant to keep God's commandments and statutes (laws) with all his heart and all his LOSU. ___ ___(___)___

The king ordered the high priest and the priests of the second order to bring the vessels for Baal and Asherah and all the other false gods out of the EEPMTL. ___ ___ ___ ___(___)___

We now know this book of law by the name UEOOETYDMNR.

(___) ___ ___ ___ ___ ___ ___ ___ ___ ___ ___

The young king gathered all the people of Judah and MUSJAELRE.

___ ___ ___ ___ ___(___)___ ___ ___

Josiah was king of HAJDU. ___ ___ ___ ___(___)

Who was the prophet who helped the young king?

___ ___ ___ ___ ___ ___ ___

Look up 2 Kings 22:14 to see if you found the correct prophet.

Josiah's Faithfulness Maze

It's not easy to stay faithful when people pressure you to act like they do. See if you can help Josiah through to the throne of righteousness.

Summer Sunday School Puzzles, © 2005 Abingdon Press

It's in the Code

Jeremiah needs helps figuring out what God's message to him is. Help him out by decoding the message below. Check your answer in the Bible (Jeremiah 1:7a).

Jeremiah was called to be a prophet when he was young—probably in his teens.

How do you think God can use young people today to carry the message to the world?

Ï Ø ‰   Á Ø ¨   Í Ó Å Ò Ò   ˝ Ø

ˇ Ø   Å Ò Ò   ˇ Ø   Œ Ó Ø Â   ˆ

Í ´ ˜ Î   Á Ø ¨   Å ˜ Î   Á Ø ¨

Í Ó Å Ò Ò   Í Π ´ Å Ô   Œ Ó Å ˇ ´ ◊ ´ ‰

ˆ   Ç Ø Â Â Å ˜ Î   Á Ø ¨

CODE

A	Å
C	Ç
D	Î
E	´
F	Ï
G	˝
H	Ó
I	^
K	Ô
L	Ò
M	Â
N	~
O	Ø
P	Π
R	‰
S	Í
T	ˇ
U	¨
V	◊
W	Œ
Y	Á

GOD'S MESSAGE

Use the Bible clues to fill in the blanks. Then write your answers in the puzzle and read God's message in the shaded letters.

The word of the LORD came to Jeremiah saying, "Before you were born I ________________ (Jeremiah 1:5) you. I appointed you a ________________ (Jeremiah 1:5) to the nations." ..."Do not say 'I am only a boy'; for you shall go to all to whom I send you, and you shall ________________ (Jeremiah 1:7) whatever I ________________ (Jeremiah 1:7) you." God's messages to Jeremiah began in the thirteenth year of King Josiah's ________________. (Jeremiah 1:2).

God said ________________ (Jeremiah 1:14) would break out on all the inhabitants of Judah unless they began to act ________________ (Jeremiah 7:5) with one another. They should not ________________ (Jeremiah 7:6) the alien, the orphan, and the widow; they should not steal, ________________ (Jeremiah 7:9), or make ________________ (Jeremiah 7:9) to other gods.

If they began to do as God required, God said, "Then I will ________________ (Jeremiah 7:7) with you...in the ________________ (Jeremiah 7:7) that I gave of old to ________________ ________________ (Jeremiah 7:7) forever and ever."

What's one message about God that you would like other people to hear?

Summer Sunday School Puzzles, © 2005 Abingdon Press

JONAH WORD SEARCH

There are nine words in this puzzle. Don't know what they should be?
Can't find them? Read the story of Jonah in your Bible.
Hint: Seven of the words appear in the Book of Jonah; two do not.

```
S  Y  A  D  J  Y  T  W
P  E  R  T  B  F  N  O
A  H  E  P  O  I  E  R
J  F  J  R  N  S  P  M
O  Q  F  E  H  H  E  F
N  S  V  A  S  T  R  H
A  E  X  C  J  Y  Z  V
H  S  I  H  S  R  A  T
```

Jonah was guilty of the sin of pride. He didn't want to save the people of Nineveh because he thought they were not worthy of it. That means that he thought he was better than the people of Nineveh.

Is there anyone that you think you are better than?

_______________   _______________   _______________

_______________   _______________   _______________

_______________   _______________   _______________

Skim through the story of Jonah in the Bible, then try to answer these questions in your own words.

1. What is Jonah's challenge?

2. What does Jonah want to do?

3. How does God respond to Jonah?

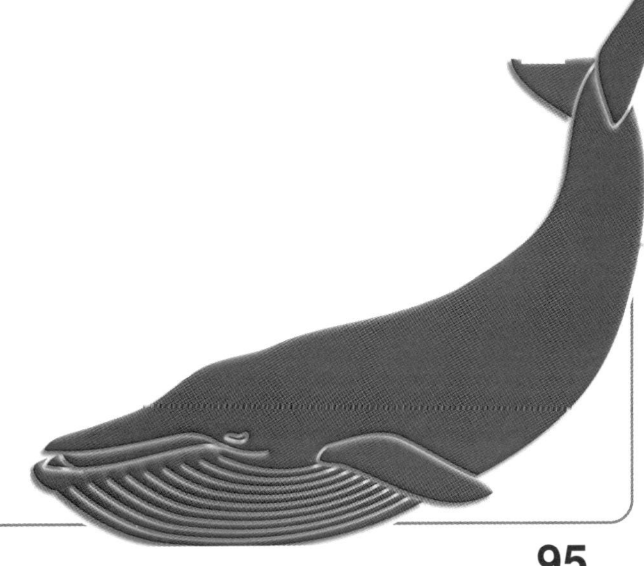

CROSSWORD

Open your Bibles to Jonah 3:1–4:5. Each word in the crossword puzzle comes from this Scripture. Read each verse and find the missing word. The Scripture references follow each clue. After you have completed the puzzle, write the circled letters on the line at the bottom of the page. Then unscramble the word to find out an important idea from today's lesson.

Across

1. Then he had a ___________ made in Nineveh. (3:7)
2. And the people of Nineveh believed God; they proclaimed a ___________. (3:5)
3. The Lord God appointed a ___________, and made it come up over Jonah. (4:6)
4. But this was very ___________ to Jonah, and he became angry. (4:1)
5. Then Jonah went out of the city and sat down east of the city, and made a ___________ for himself there. (4:5)

Down

1. ___________ ___________ more, and Nineveh shall be overthrown! (3:4b)
2. Who knows? God may ___________ and change his mind. (3:9)
3. God appointed a ___________ that attacked the bush. (4:7)
4. The word of the Lord came to ___________ a second time. (3:1)
5. Everyone, great and small, put on ___________. (3:5b)
6. "Get up, go to ___________, that great city." (3:2)

Why do you think God wanted to save the people of Nineveh?

Who's a Prophet?

The prophets in the Hebrew Scriptures were called by God to call the people back to obedience to God. Each of these prophets was called directly to influence a king of Judah or Israel.

Many of the people listed below are considered Old Testament prophets. The others are not prophets. Put a "P" on the line in front of the Old Testament prophets. If the person is not an Old Testament prophet, put an "X" and write on the line behind the name what "profession" the person had—it might even be "New Testament Prophet." Choose from the list of titles provided and use the Table of Contents and other helps in your Bible to help you where you need help.

Helpful Hint: The books of the prophets often start with how the prophet was called by God.

___Isaiah _______________________   ___Saul _______________________

___John the Baptist ______________   ___David ______________________

___Matthew _____________________   ___Micah ______________________

___Jeremiah ____________________   ___Nathan _____________________

___Amos _______________________   ___Habakkuk ___________________

___Ezekiel ______________________   ___Zephaniah __________________

___Luke ________________________   ___Haggai _____________________

___Deborah _____________________   ___Esther _____________________

___Daniel ______________________   ___Zechariah __________________

___Hosea ______________________   ___Malachi ____________________

___Paul ________________________   ___Huldah ____________________

___Jonah _______________________   ___Ruth ______________________

___Joel ________________________

___Josiah ______________________

___Obadiah_____________________

Possible professions: king, queen, gleaner, judge, tentmaker (Apostle), Old Testament prophet, New Testament prophet, physician, tax collector (Apostle).

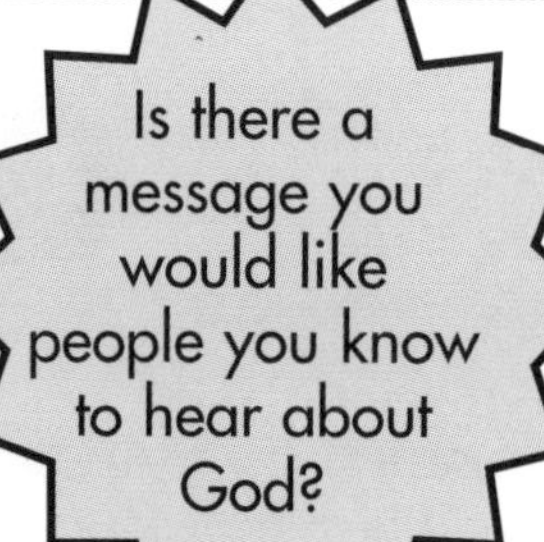

Mix and Match

Cut apart the cards below, then quickly try to match the prophet with his message. Scripture references are given so you can look them up in your Bible if necessary.

I will heal their disloyalty: I will love them freely, for my anger has turned from them.	Let justice roll down like waters, and righteousness like an ever-flowing stream.
I will put my law within them, and I will write it on their hearts; and I will be their God, and they shall be my people.	Do not say, 'I am only a boy'; for you shall go to all to whom I send you, and you shall speak whatever I command you.
If you do not stand firm in faith, you shall not stand at all.	The Lord GOD has spoken; who can but prophesy?
The LORD indeed is God; the LORD indeed is God.	He has told you, O mortal, what is good; and what does the LORD require of you but to do justice, and to love kindness, and to walk humbly with your God?
Isaiah 7:9b	(Elijah) 1 Kings 18:39b	Amos 3:8b	Jeremiah 1:7
Hosea 14:4	Amos 5:24	Jeremiah 31:33b	Micah 6:8

Mixed-Up Letters

When a woman in Bethany anointed Jesus, the disciples were upset. Follow the directions to discover the words that Jesus said regarding her action. Check Matthew 26:13 to see if you're right.

Change every Z to O
Change every C to R
Change every X to N
Change every O to T
Change every W to B
Change every D to M
Change every E to D
Change every U to Y
Change every T to C
Change every K to V
Change every G to A

Change every L to I
Change every Q to P
Change every A to L
Change every V to F
Change every Y to U
Change every P to S
Change every N to H
Change every F to W
Change every J to E
Change every B to G

O C Y A U   L   O J A A   U Z Y ,

F N J C J K J C   O N L P

B Z Z E   X J F P   L P

Q C Z T A G L D J E   L X

O N J   F N Z A J   F Z C A E ,

F N G O   P N J   N G P

E Z X J   F L A A   W J   O Z A E   L X

C J D J D W C G X T J Z V   N J C .

Gospel Comparison

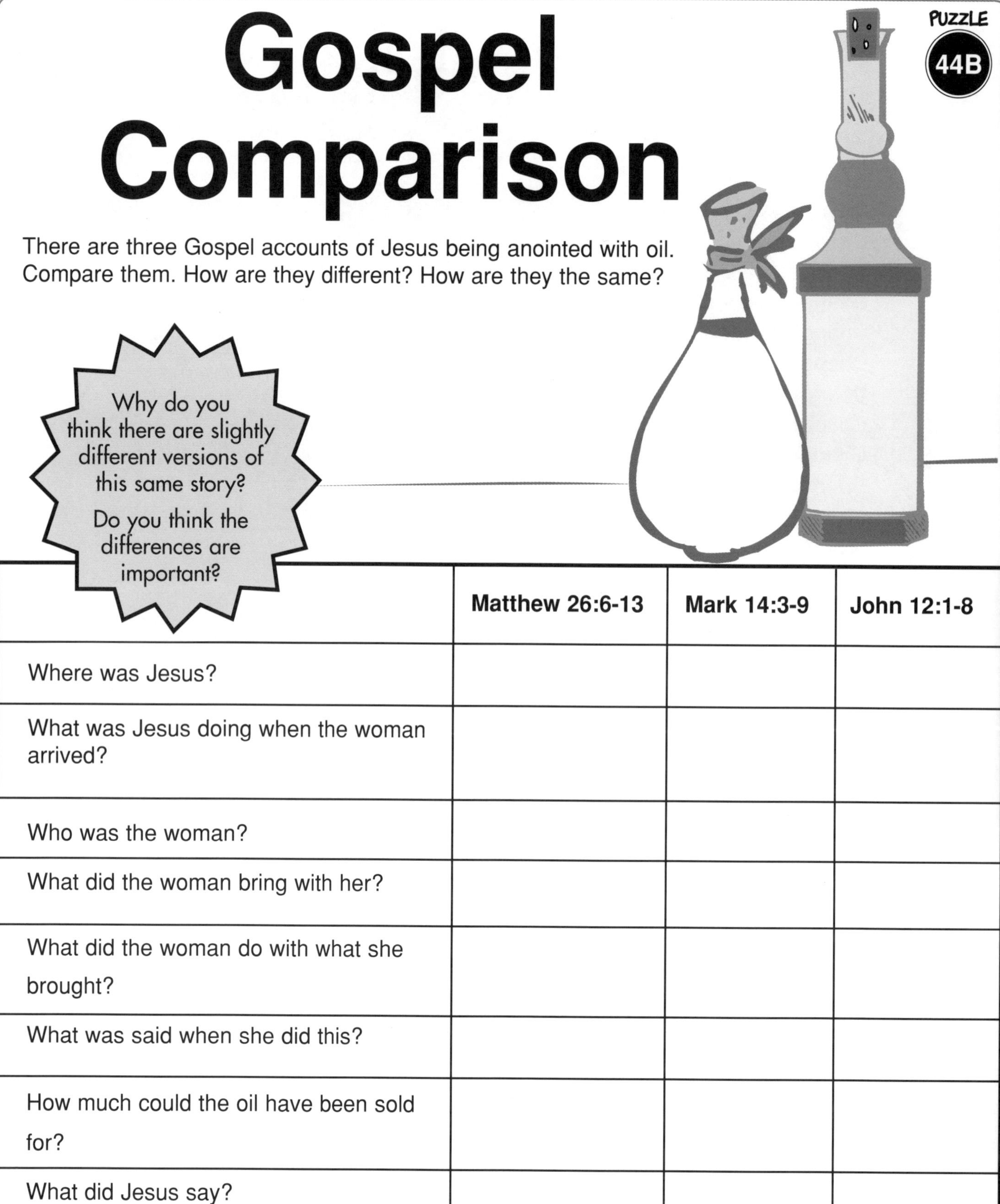

There are three Gospel accounts of Jesus being anointed with oil. Compare them. How are they different? How are they the same?

Why do you think there are slightly different versions of this same story?

Do you think the differences are important?

	Matthew 26:6-13	Mark 14:3-9	John 12:1-8
Where was Jesus?			
What was Jesus doing when the woman arrived?			
Who was the woman?			
What did the woman bring with her?			
What did the woman do with what she brought?			
What was said when she did this?			
How much could the oil have been sold for?			
What did Jesus say?			
What will be remembered?			

Great Friends

Once four friends believed in Jesus enough to overcome some great obstacles in order to get a friend in need to Jesus. They lowered the man though the roof to Jesus, and because of their faith Jesus cured the man. Solve the code, put the words in the correct order, and find out what Jesus said to the man (Mark 2:5).

Famous Friends

There were some famous friends in the Bible. See if you can draw lines to match up the friends below. Be careful—some of them are friends with more than one of the others.

Jesus	David	Pilate	Timothy
Shadrach	Meshach	Zophar	Daniel
Herod	Peter	James	man who was paralyzed
Jonathan	John	Paul/Saul	
Abednego	Job	Eliphaz	Bildad
Barnabas			four friends with a pallet

Having trouble? Maybe these Scripture passages can help:

I Samuel 20:1	Job 2:11
Daniel 1:7	Matthew 17:1
Mark 2:3	Luke 23:12
Acts 13:1-2	Acts 16:3a

Think of your best friend. How important is it to your friendship that you believe a lot of the same things?

Summer Sunday School Puzzles, © 2005 Abingdon Press

Where's Haman?

In the Book of Esther there is a man named Haman who tries to trick the king into hanging Mordecai, Esther's cousin. The king is very angry with Haman. Haman has put on a disguise and is hiding out. Pretend that you are the person sent to arrest Haman. Because of his disguise you can't recognize him. There are witnesses who might help you, but they don't know you, and don't know if they should trust your story about the king's anger. **In describing Haman each person tells you one thing that is true and one thing that is false.**

Review their testimony, decide which person below is Haman, and draw a circle around him.

Witness #1:
Haman has a beard and is wearing a short robe.

Witness #2:
Haman is clean-shaven with gold chains around his neck.

Witness #3:
Haman is wearing a long robe and has a sash as his belt.

Witness #4:
Haman is wearing sandals and wears a sword in a scabbard.

Decode a Verse

In a difficult situation, Queen Esther and her relative Mordecai were able to save the lives of the Hebrews. Decode the Bible verse below to find out more about finding good things in difficult situations.

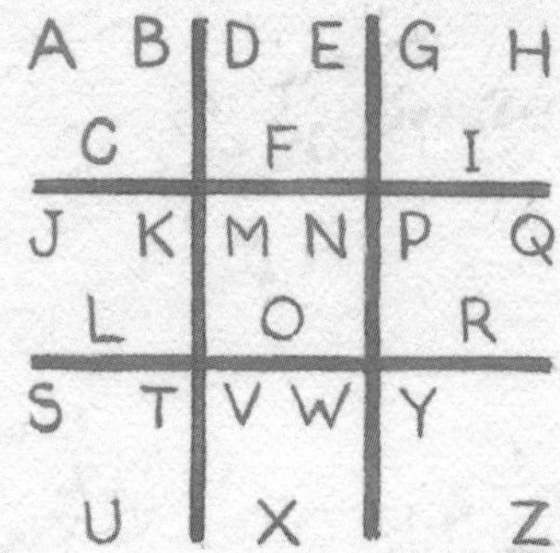

(________ 8:28)

104

Summer Sunday School Puzzles, © 2005 Abingdon Press

Justice Scale Puzzle

Use the coded letters in the honesty words to discover the Bible verse at the bottom of the page.

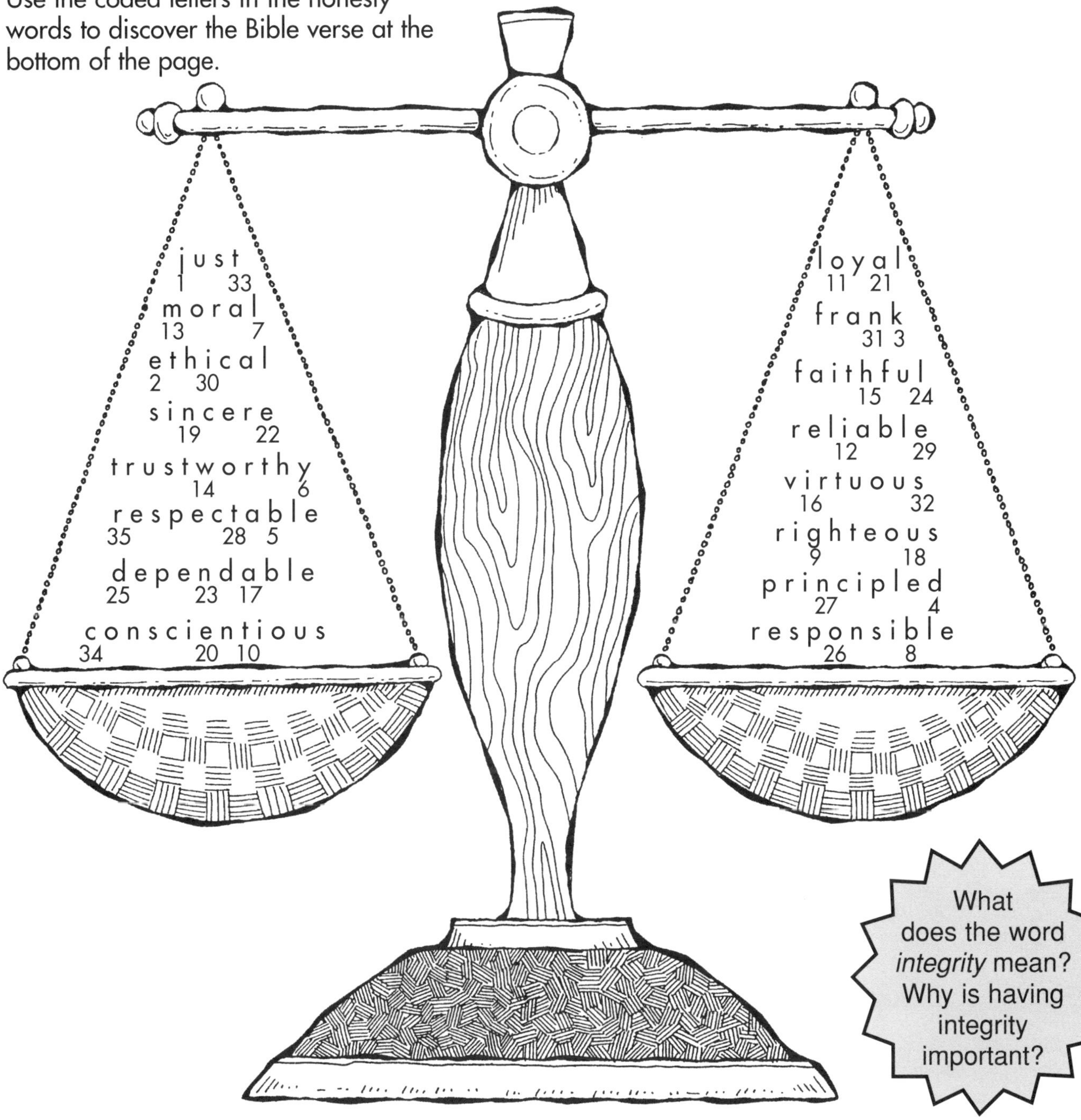

Left scale (honesty words):

just
1   33

moral
13   7

ethical
2   30

sincere
19   22

trustworthy
14   6

respectable
35   28 5

dependable
25   23 17

conscientious
34   20 10

Right scale (honesty words):

loyal
11 21

frank
31 3

faithful
15   24

reliable
12   29

virtuous
16   32

righteous
9   18

principled
27   4

responsible
26   8

What does the word *integrity* mean? Why is having integrity important?

Our hope and prayer is that we can live a life pleasing to God so that God may do the following:

"___ ___ ___   ___ ___ ___ ___   ___ ___ ___ ___ ___ ___   ___ ___ ___   ___ ___ ___ ___   ___ ___ ___ ___ ___ ___ ___'
 7 2 10   13 20 8 29   14 2 30 9 15 20 4   16 31   17   1 18 32 33   5 21 7 17 19 34 22

___ ___ ___   ___ ___ ___   ___ ___ ___   ___ ___ ___   ___ ___   ___ ___ ___ ___ ___ ___ ___ ___ ___ ___!" *(Job 31:6)*
21 23 25   24 2 10   9 11 25   3 23 26 14   13 6   12 27 28 2 9 35 30 28 6

In a Swirl

Start at the middle of the puzzle and write down every other letter to find Job 38:4.

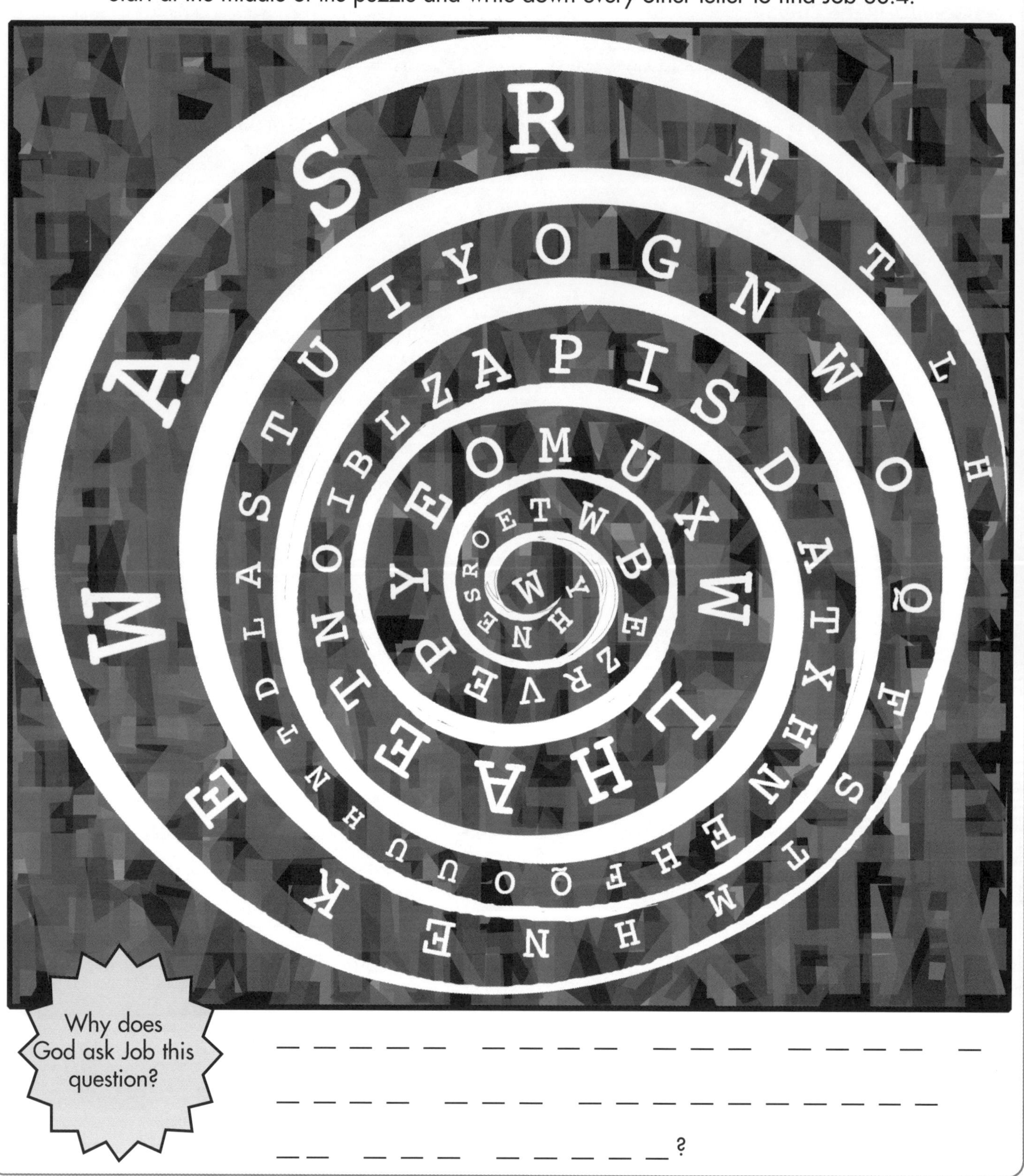

___ ___ ___ ___ ___ ___ ___ ___ ___ ___

___ ___ ___ ___ ___ ___ ___ ___ ___

___ ___ ___ ___ ___ ___ ___ ?

Summer Sunday School Puzzles, © 2005 Abingdon Press

DANIEL 6:16B

Use the grid below to decode today's Bible verse. Each letter is a pair of numbers. For example, if the clue is *22*: Look for the first number, 2, in the column on the left. Then look for the second number, 2, in the column across the top. Find the letter in the grid where the rows for 2 and 2 intersect, which in this case will be "F." Write the letter "F" above the number 22. Continue until you have found all the letters that belong in the puzzle.

Hint: The number 73 indicates a comma, and the number 74 indicates a space between words.

	1	2	3	4
1	A	B	C	D
2	E	F	G	H
3	I	J	K	L
4	M	N	O	P
5	Q	R	S	T
6	U	V	W	X
7	Y	Z	,	

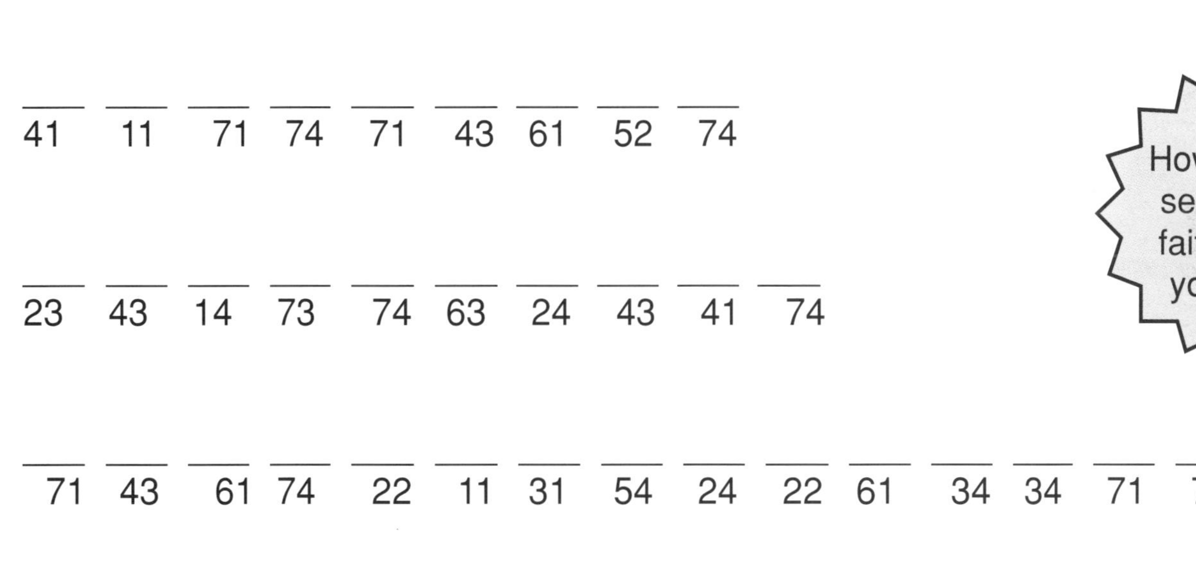

```
___ ___ ___ ___ ___ ___ ___ ___ ___
41  11  71  74  71  43  61  52  74

___ ___ ___ ___ ___ ___ ___ ___ ___ ___
23  43  14  73  74  63  24  43  41  74
```

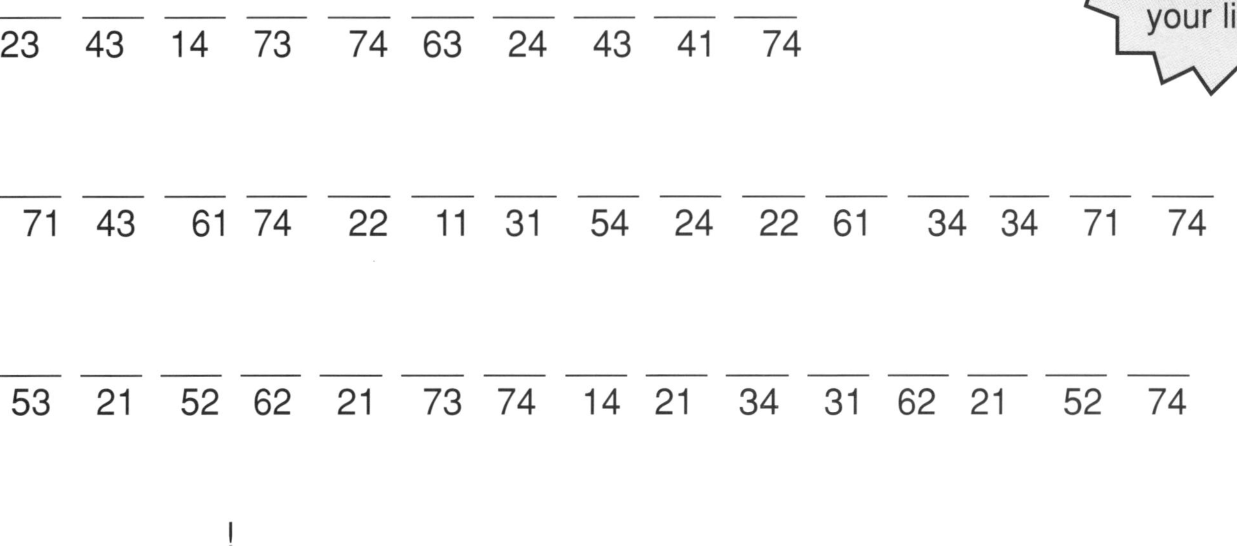

```
___ ___ ___ ___ ___ ___ ___ ___ ___ ___ ___ ___ ___ ___ ___
71  43  61  74  22  11  31  54  24  22  61  34  34  71  74

___ ___ ___ ___ ___ ___ ___ ___ ___ ___ ___ ___ ___ ___ ___
53  21  52  62  21  73  74  14  21  34  31  62  21  52  74

___ ___ ___!
71  43  61
```

How do you serve God faithfully in your life?

Testing of Faith

Daniel's faith in God was put to the test. In the Bible there are many people whose faith was put to the test. Match the people or groups below with how they were tested.

	staying at home with family or traveling with Paul
Disciples	
	fiery furnace
Stephen	
	crucifixion of Jesus
Paul	
	possible destruction of the Jewish people
Daniel	
Shadrach, Meshach, and Abednego	stoning
Job	loss of everything and everyone he loved
Esther	
	taking God's message of salvation to a group of people he didn't want saved
Ruth	arrested, shipwrecked, tried
Jonah	
	lion's den
Timothy	
	leaving home country for a foreign land

Abigail, Peacemaker

Look up the verses in your Bible of the story of Abigail and David and fill in the numbers.

Nabal owned [______] sheep and [______] goats. (1 Samuel 25:2)

David sent [______] young men to greet Nabal. (1 Samuel 25:5)

David also strapped on his sword; and about [______] men went up after David, while [______] remained with the baggage. (1 Samuel 25:13)

But [______] of the young men told Abigail, Nabal's wife. (1 Samuel 25:14)

Then Abigail hurried and took [______] loaves, [______] skins of wine, [______] sheep ready dressed, [______] measures of parched grain, [______] clusters of raisins, and [______] cakes of figs. (1 Samuel 25:18)

For as surely as the Lord the God of Israel lives, who has restrained me from hurting you, unless you had hurried and come to meet me, truly by morning there would not have been left to Nabal so much as [______] male. (1 Samuel 25:34)

Use Your Bible

What is one thing you are glad to tell others about God?

Use your Bible to find words that help achieve peace. (A letter has been filled in for each word; you can work back and forth between the alphabet and the letters.) Look up the verses in the Bible to check your answers!

Hebrews 9:15 ___ ___ ___ ___ ___ ___ ___ R
10 25 3 24 26 16 23

Matthew 9:36 ___ O ___ ___ ___ ___ ___ ___ ___ ___
2 10 12 26 15 15 24 23 11

Ephesians 1:7 F ___ ___ ___ ___ ___ ___ ___ ___ ___
23 14 5 24 17 25 11 25 15 15

Romans 11:15 ___ ___ ___ ___ ___ T ___ ___ ___ ___
26 2 2 25 12 26 11 2 25

Hebrews 12:9 R ___ ___ ___ ___ ___ ___
25 15 12 25 2 16

Galatians 5:23 ___ ___ ___ ___ - C ___ ___ ___ ___ ___ ___
15 25 9 4 23 11 16 14 23 9

Proverbs 2:2 ___ ___ ___ ___ ___ ___ ___ ___ ___ ___ ___ G
22 11 3 25 14 15 16 26 11 3 24 11

Proverbs 1:7 W ___ ___ ___ ___ ___
24 15 3 23 10

Proverbs 23:22 ___ ___ ___ ___ ___ N
9 24 15 16 25

Use the numbers to look up the letters that spell out four more peace producers.

___ ___ ___ ___ ___ ___ E ___ ___ ___ ___ ___
24 11 16 25 14 17 11 16 24 23 11

C ___ ___ ___ ___ ___ ___ ___ ___ ___
23 23 12 25 14 26 16 24 23 11

___ O ___ ___ ___ ___ ___ ___ ___ ___
2 10 12 14 23 10 24 15 25

___ ___ ___ ___ ___ H ___
25 10 12 26 16 21

Alphabet key:
A=26 B=1 C=2 D=3 E=25 F=4 G=5 H=6 I=24 J=7 K=8 L=9 M=10 N=11 O=12 P=23 Q=13 R=15 S=16 T=17 U=22 V=18 W=19 X=21 Y=20 Z=20

Amos 5:24

Amos was a prophet of God with an important message. To discover the message, follow the directions carefully. Check your work by reading Amos 5:24.

Cross out all words that begin with "f."
Cross out all words that contain two of the same vowels side by side.
Cross out all words that begin with "i."
Cross out all words that name a type of sporting equipment

Write the remaining words on the lines below (in order please).

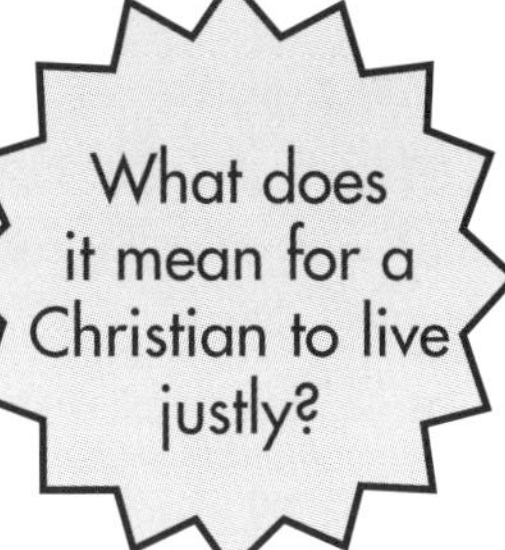

racket   fuel   seen   let   skateboard   bee   justice

roll   down   fair   like   boat   waters   and

basketball   island   righteousness   feel   like   fine

booth   final   inline skates   individual   bike   an   ball

ice   bicycle   sleeping   ever-flowing   net   eel   stream

door   fun   bat   friend   Aarron   helmet   between

__ __ __   __ __ __   __ __ __

__ __ __ __ __ __   __ __ __ __ __ __ ,

__ __ __   __ __ __ __ __ __ __ __ __

__ __ __ __   __ __ __ __ __ __ __ __ __ __

__ __ __ __ __ __ .

WHAT DOESN'T BELONG?

Learn some things about one of the people in the Old Testament by deciding which item in the groups below doesn't belong. Circle the word that is different. When you finish, you will know more about this person than you did when you started.

1. king   queen   prophet   prince

2. David   Solomon   Saul   Amos

3. Jerusalem   Tekoa   Judah   Jericho

4. rocket scientist   computer programmer   shepherd   airline pilot

5. war   theft   justice   lying

Summer Sunday School Puzzles, © 2005 Abingdon Press

Micah's Poem

Micah spoke out for God, telling the people that if they did not learn to live with justice and kindness, disaster would come. God also gave Micah a message of hope, so Micah composed a poem. Read Micah's poem in Micah 4:1-4, then complete the sentences below.

1. God will ________________ the people God's way.

2. When the nations cannot agree, God will ________________ their disputes.

3. Nations will beat their swords into ________________ .

4. People will hammer their ________________ into pruning hooks.

5. People will not learn ________________ any more.

Use the answers above to fill in the blanks below. Write the words in order (1-5).

What does it mean to beat swords into plowshares?

Unscramble the boxed letters and you will learn what Micah's poem was about.

MATCH THE WORD WITH THE MEANING

plowshare

going against the will of God

arbitrate

a forked stick with a pointed metal tip used for breaking up the ground

pruning hook

a gift given to God as an act of worship

transgression

a curved blade attached to a handle, used for removing twigs and trimming vines

offering

to judge or to make a decision regarding a dispute

Name one way people today could change from using a weapon to doing something peaceful and for the good of all.

Jesus' Words About Justice

Jesus had a lot to say about how we should treat others justly. Fill in the blanks below using the words provided to discover just a few of the things Jesus taught us about justice. If you have any trouble, look up the Bible references.

Which of these instructions is the hardest to follow? Why?

Note: A word may be used more than once.

1. Do not __________, so that you may not be ____________. (Matthew 7:1)

2. In everything ____ to __________ as you would have ________ _______ to you. (Matthew 7:12) BONUS: What is this saying called? ____________________________

3. Blessed are the ______________, for they will receive ______________. (Matthew 5:7) BONUS: This comes from a group of similar sayings that is called? ____________________.

4. I say to you, _________ your ___________ and _________ for those who ________________ you. (Matthew 5:44)

5. Whoever wants to be ___________ must be ______ ______ _________ and _____________ of all. (Mark 9:35b)

6. Whoever ________________ one such ___________ in my name ________________ me, and whoever ________________ me ________________ not me but the _________ who ___________ me. (Mark 9:37)

7. ___________ my ___________. (John 21:17c)

all	first	love	sent
child	them	merciful	servant
pray	judge	mercy	sheep
do	welcomes	of	persecute
enemies	judged	one	
feed	last	others	

Building Stones
for Life

The wall below represents some of the qualities of good building blocks that are needed for a faithful Christian life. Unscramble the letters on each stone to determine the quality.

Summer Sunday School Puzzles, © 2005 Abingdon Press

Puzzle Answers

Answers—Old Testament Puzzles

PUZZLE 1—Serpent in the Garden

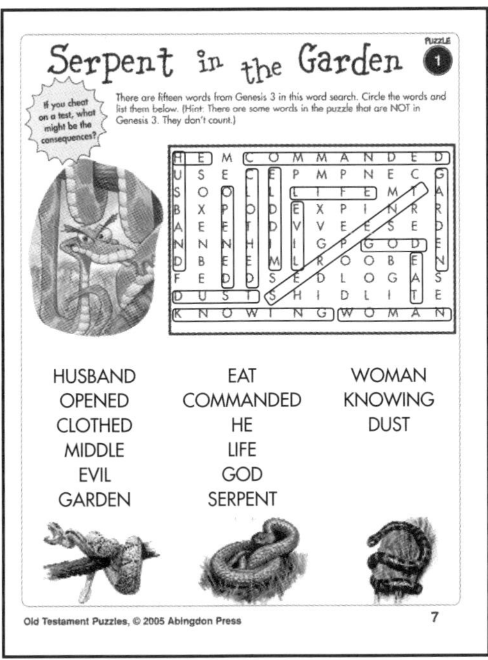

PUZZLE 1B—Curious Caleb's Confused Creation

1. On the sixth day.
2. Dominion.
3. Not to eat from the tree of knowledge of good and evil.
4. The serpent.
5. God told them not to do it.
6. Before.
7. God rested.
8. Adam.
9. God created the heavens and the earth on the first day.
10. "Let there be light."

PUZZLE 2—Who? What? How?

1. Cain.
2. Abel kept sheep, and Cain was a tiller of the ground.
3. Cain frowned.
4. C
5. Cain killed Abel.
6. "Where is your brother Abel?"

PUZZLE 2B—Questioning Alphabet

AM I MY BROTHER'S KEEPER?

PUZZLE 3—Tower of Words

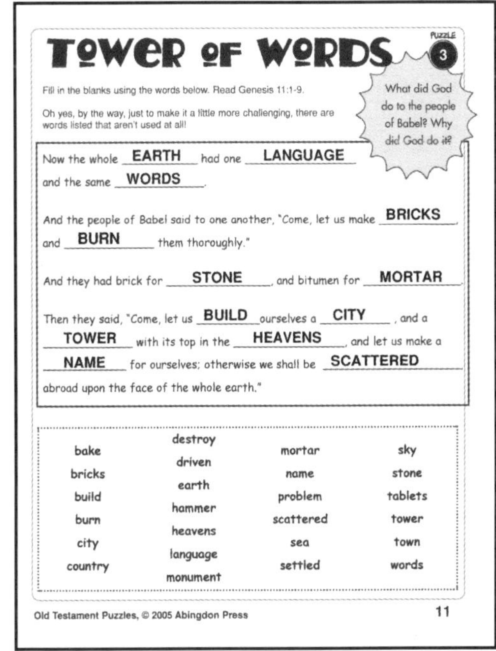

PUZZLE 3B—Tower of Babel

DO NOTHING FROM SELFISH AMBITION OR CONCEIT.

PUZZLE 4—Map for Peace

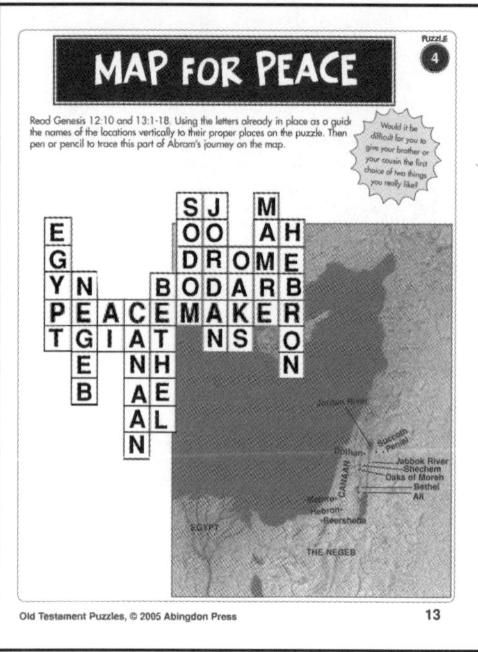

PUZZLE 4B—Decode a Bible Verse

LET THERE BE NO STRIFE BETWEEN YOU AND ME, AND BETWEEN YOUR HERDERS AND MY HERDERS; FOR WE ARE KINDRED. IS NOT THE WHOLE LAND BEFORE YOU? SEPARATE YOURSELF FROM ME. IF YOU TAKE THE LEFT HAND, THEN I WILL GO TO THE RIGHT; OR IF YOU TAKE THE RIGHT HAND, THEN I WILL GO TO THE LEFT.

PUZZLE 5—A Proverb

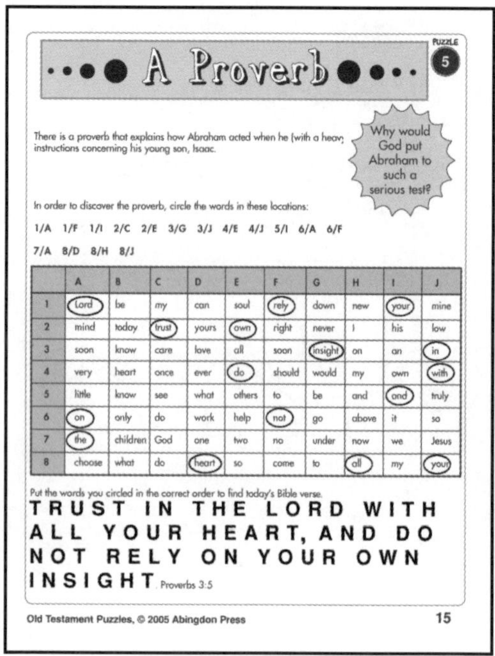

	A	B	C	D	E	F	G	H	I	J
1	Lord	be	my	can	soul	rely	down	new	your	mine
2	mind	today	trust	yours	own	right	never	I	his	low
3	soon	know	care	love	all	soon	insight	on	an	in
4	very	heart	once	ever	do	should	would	my	own	with
5	little	know	see	what	others	to	be	and	and	truly
6	on	only	do	work	help	not	go	above	it	so
7	the	children	God	one	two	no	under	now	we	Jesus
8	choose	what	do	heart	so	come	to	all	my	your

PUZZLE 5B—Monotheism

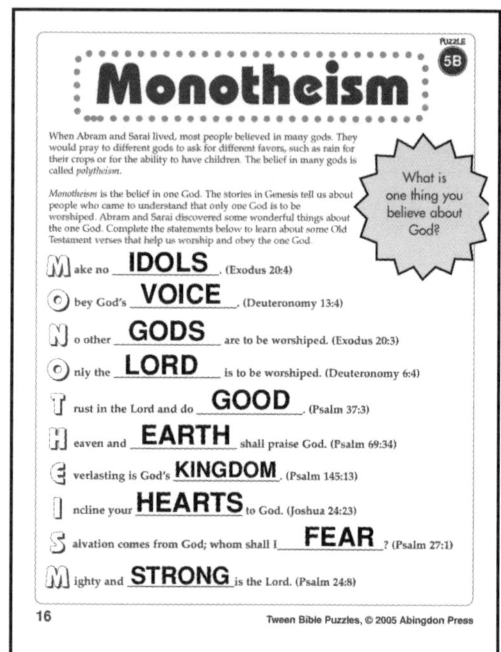

Puzzle 6—The Not So Good Deal

Esau sold his **BIRTHRIGHT** for **STEW**.

Puzzle Answers

PUZZLE 6B—What's True? What's Not?

1. The parents of Jacob and Esau were Abraham and Sarah.	F
2. Jacob and Esau were twins.	T
3. Esau was the older brother.	T
4. The older brother was the one who would inherit the blessing.	T
5. Jacob was told by a close friend how to deceive his father.	F
6. Jacob's father was almost blind, so Jacob put hairy skins on his arms so that his father would think he was Esau.	T
7. Jacob's father believed the deception right away.	F
8. Isaac gave Esau's blessing to Jacob.	T
9. Because of the stolen blessing, Esau got nothing.	F
10. Jacob lived happily ever after on the family estate.	F

PUZZLE 7—Map Work

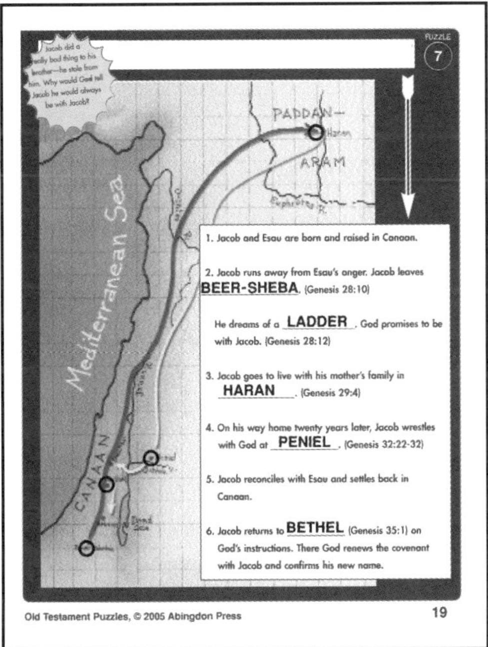

PUZZLE 7B—What Would Jacob's Name Be From Now On?

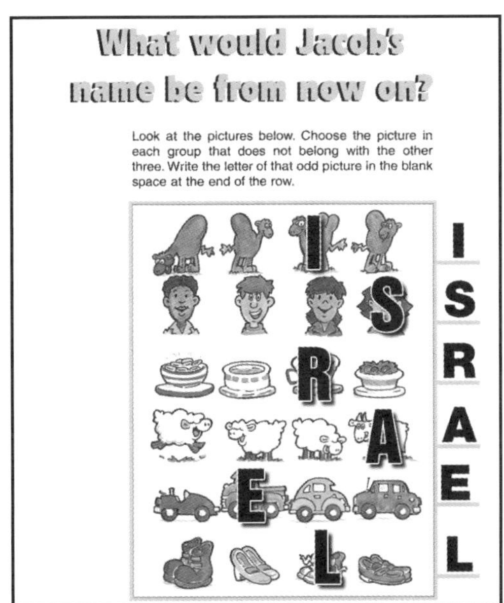

PUZZLE 8—Where Do You Go?

GOD IS OUR REFUGE AND STRENGTH, A VERY PRESENT HELP IN TROUBLE.

PUZZLE 8B—The Hebrew Family Travels

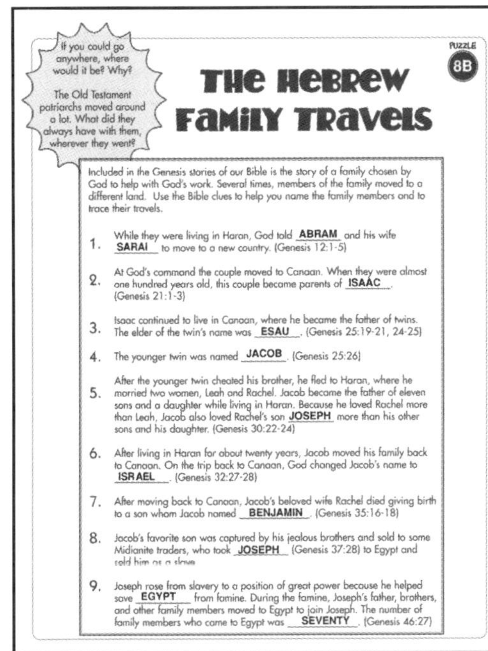

PUZZLE 9—Hidden Message

WHERE CAN I GO FROM YOUR SPIRIT? OR WHERE CAN I FLEE FROM YOUR PRESENCE?

PUZZLE 9B—What Belongs? What Doesn't?

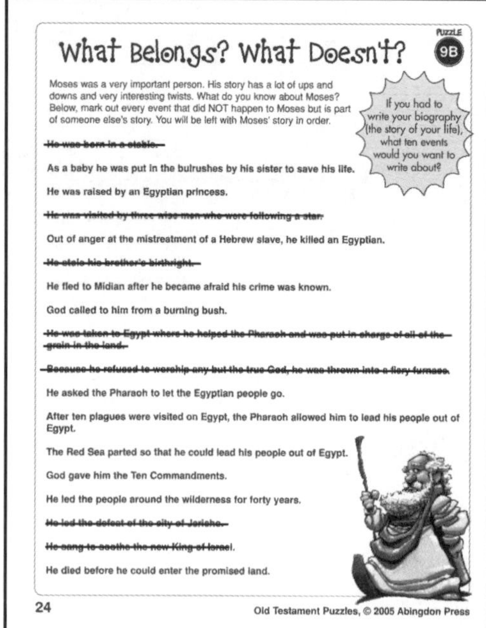

What Belongs? What Doesn't?

PUZZLE 10—Deborah, the Judge

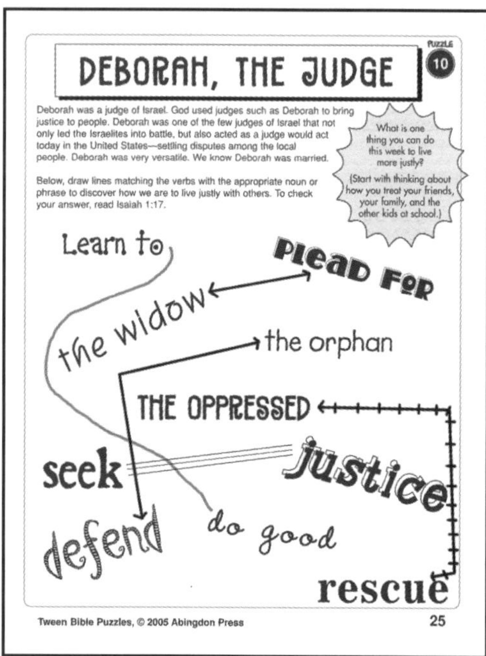

Puzzle 10B—Women in the Bible

PUZZLE 11—Important People in Saul's Life

PUZZLE 11B—Go Figure!

$48 \div 6 = \underline{8}$　　$8 \times 9 = \underline{72}$
$\underline{8} + 3 = \underline{11}$　　$72 - 42 = \underline{30}$
$\underline{11} \times 3 = \underline{33}$　　$\underline{30} \div 15 = \underline{2}$

Read Psalm **33:2** to find that the lyre (or harp) David would have used has **10** strings.

PUZZLE 12—David's Web of Sin

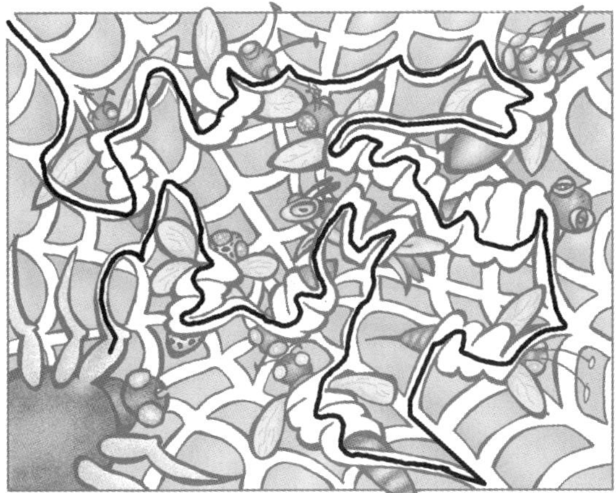

1. Bathsheba
2. adultery
3. Uriah; be killed
4. Bathsheba
5. Nathan; parable
6. repents
7. forgiven; consequence

PUZZLE 12B—Coded Psalm

PUZZLE 13—Amos's Words About Justice

LET JUSTICE ROLL DOWN LIKE WATERS, AND RIGHTEOUSNESS LIKE AN EVER-FLOWING STREAM.

PUZZLE 13B—From One Beginning to the Next

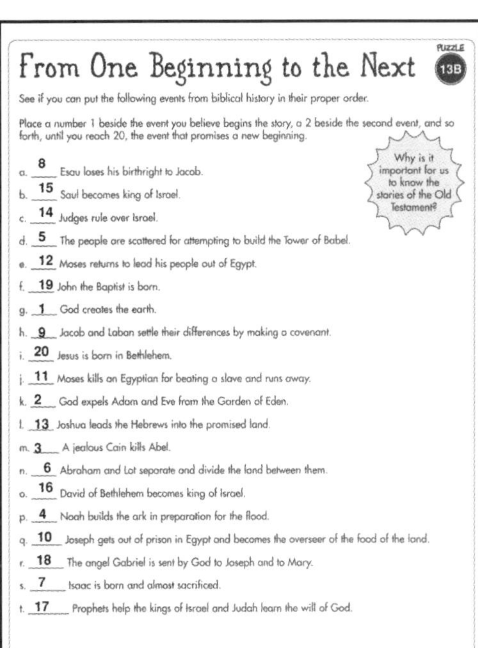

From One Beginning to the Next

See if you can put the following events from biblical history in their proper order.

Place a number 1 beside the event you believe begins the story, a 2 beside the second event, and so forth, until you reach 20, the event that promises a new beginning.

a. __8__ Esau loses his birthright to Jacob.
b. __15__ Saul becomes king of Israel.
c. __14__ Judges rule over Israel.
d. __5__ The people are scattered for attempting to build the Tower of Babel.
e. __12__ Moses returns to lead his people out of Egypt.
f. __19__ John the Baptist is born.
g. __1__ God creates the earth.
h. __9__ Jacob and Laban settle their differences by making a covenant.
i. __20__ Jesus is born in Bethlehem.
j. __11__ Moses kills an Egyptian for beating a slave and runs away.
k. __2__ God expels Adam and Eve from the Garden of Eden.
l. __13__ Joshua leads the Hebrews into the promised land.
m. __3__ A jealous Cain kills Abel.
n. __6__ Abraham and Lot separate and divide the land between them.
o. __16__ David of Bethlehem becomes king of Israel.
p. __4__ Noah builds the ark in preparation for the flood.
q. __10__ Joseph gets out of prison in Egypt and becomes the overseer of the food of the land.
r. __18__ The angel Gabriel is sent by God to Joseph and to Mary.
s. __7__ Isaac is born and almost sacrificed.
t. __17__ Prophets help the kings of Israel and Judah learn the will of God.

Why is it important for us to know the stories of the Old Testament?

Answers—New Testament Puzzles (Part 1)

PUZZLE 14—Scattered Words

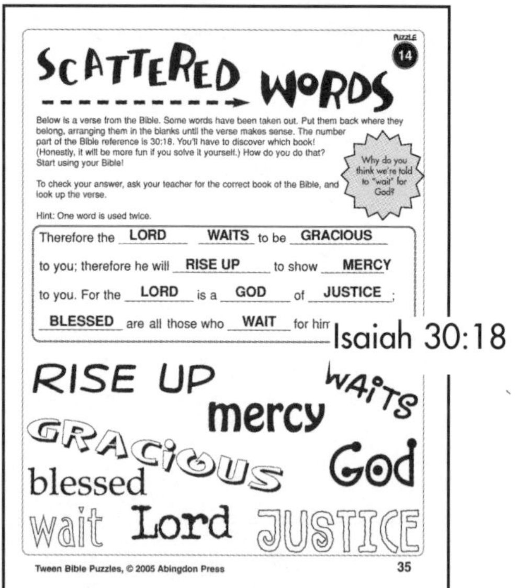

PUZZLE 14B—Quote Fall

PUZZLE 15—Color It Puzzle

PUZZLE 15B—Name Game

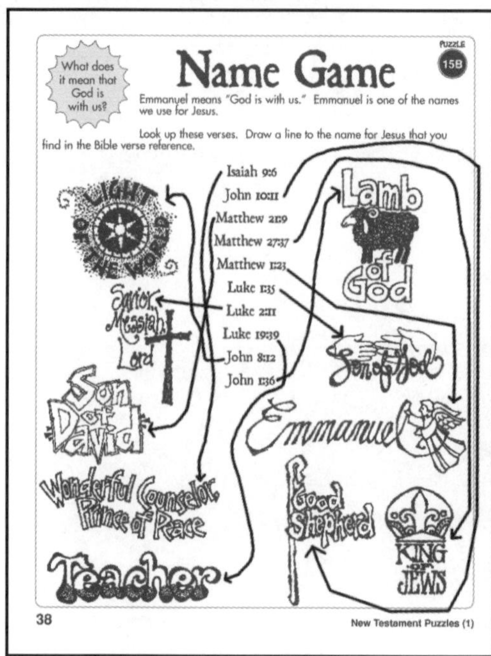

PUZZLE 16—In Those Days

PUZZLE 16B—Christmas Timeline

- An angel tells Mary she will have a child.
- An angel visits Joseph in a dream.
- Augustus Caesar orders the people to go to their hometowns to be registered.
- Mary and Joseph go to Bethlehem for the census.
- Jesus is born.
- Shepherds visit Jesus in the stable.
- Simeon and Anna see baby Jesus when he is presented at the Temple.
- The wise men stop to see King Herod.
- Herod seeks out the baby Jesus to kill him.
- Mary and Joseph take the baby Jesus and flee to Egypt.

PUZZLE 17—A Few Crosswords for the Shepherds

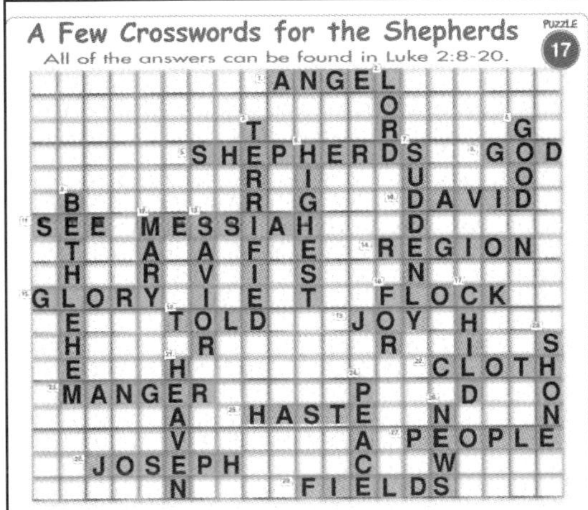

PUZZLE 17B—Shepherd Squares

PUZZLE 18—Epiphany Exam

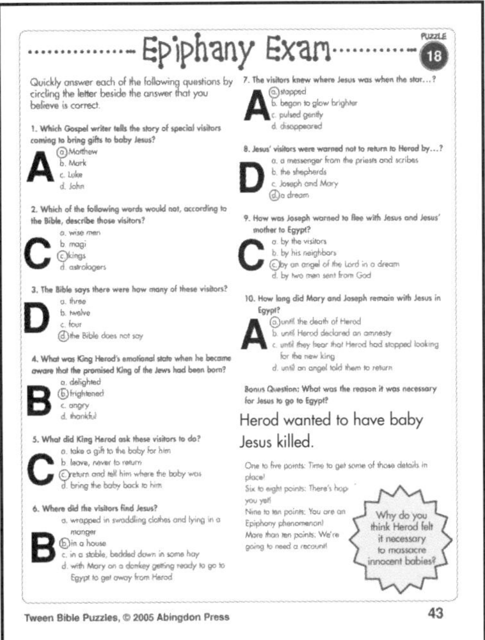

············· Epiphany Exam ············· PUZZLE 18

Quickly answer each of the following questions by circling the letter beside the answer that you believe is correct.

1. Which Gospel writer tells the story of special visitors coming to bring gifts to baby Jesus?

A
a. Matthew
b. Mark
c. Luke
d. John

2. Which of the following words would not, according to the Bible, describe those visitors?

C
a. wise men
b. magi
c. kings
d. astrologers

3. The Bible says there were how many of these visitors?

D
a. three
b. twelve
c. four
d. the Bible does not say

4. What was King Herod's emotional state when he became aware that the promised King of the Jews had been born?

B
a. delighted
b. frightened
c. angry
d. thankful

5. What did King Herod ask these visitors to do?

C
a. take a gift to the baby for him
b. leave, never to return
c. return and tell him where the baby was
d. bring the baby back to him

6. Where did the visitors find Jesus?

B
a. wrapped in swaddling clothes and lying in a manger
b. in a house
c. in a stable, bedded down in some hay
d. with Mary on a donkey getting ready to go to Egypt to get away from Herod

7. The visitors knew where Jesus was when the star…?

A
a. stopped
b. began to glow brighter
c. pulsed gently
d. disappeared

8. Jesus' visitors were warned not to return to Herod by…?

D
a. a messenger from the priests and scribes
b. the shepherds
c. Joseph and Mary
d. a dream

9. How was Joseph warned to flee with Jesus and Jesus' mother to Egypt?

C
a. by the visitors
b. by his neighbors
c. by an angel of the Lord in a dream
d. by two men sent from God

10. How long did Mary and Joseph remain with Jesus in Egypt?

A
a. until the death of Herod
b. until Herod declared an amnesty
c. until they hear that Herod had stopped looking for the new king
d. until an angel told them to return

Bonus Question: What was the reason it was necessary for Jesus to go to Egypt?

Herod wanted to have baby Jesus killed.

One to five points: Time to get some of those details in place!
Six to eight points: There's hope you yet!
Nine to ten points: You are an Epiphany phenomenon!
More than ten points: We're going to need a recount!

Why do you think Herod felt it necessary to massacre innocent babies?

Tween Bible Puzzles, © 2005 Abingdon Press

43

PUZZLE 18B—The Search

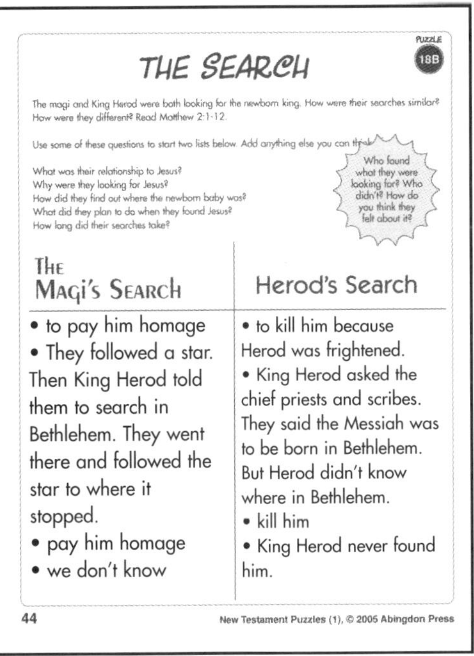

THE SEARCH

PUZZLE 18B

The magi and King Herod were both looking for the newborn king. How were their searches similar? How were they different? Read Matthew 2:1-12.

Use some of these questions to start two lists below. Add anything else you can think.

What was their relationship to Jesus?
Why were they looking for Jesus?
How did they find out where the newborn baby was?
What did they plan to do when they found Jesus?
How long did their searches take?

Who found what they were looking for? Who didn't? How do you think they felt about it?

THE MAGI'S SEARCH	Herod's Search
• to pay him homage • They followed a star. Then King Herod told them to search in Bethlehem. They went there and followed the star to where it stopped. • pay him homage • we don't know	• to kill him because Herod was frightened. • King Herod asked the chief priests and scribes. They said the Messiah was to be born in Bethlehem. But Herod didn't know where in Bethlehem. • kill him • King Herod never found him.

44   New Testament Puzzles (1), © 2005 Abingdon Press

PUZZLE 19—Remember These

One does not live by bread alone, but by every word that comes from the mouth of God. (Matthew 4:4)

Do not put the Lord your God to the test. (Matthew 4:7)

Away with you, Satan! (Matthew 4:10a)

Worship the Lord your God, and serve only him. (Matthew 4:10b)

Repent, for the kingdom of heaven has come near. (Matthew 4:17)

PUZZLE 19B—Sacrament

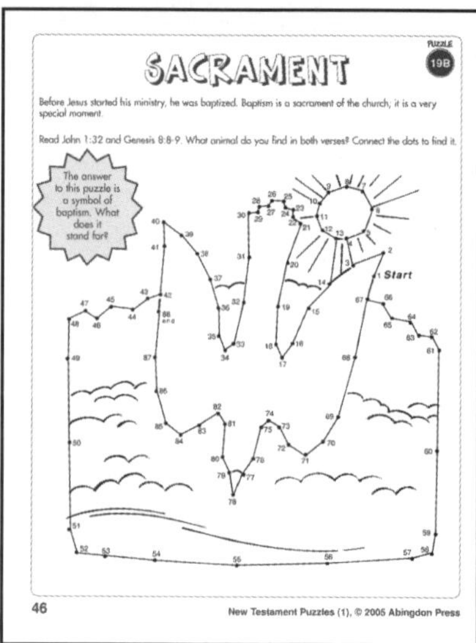

PUZZLE 20—Mystery Word Puzzle

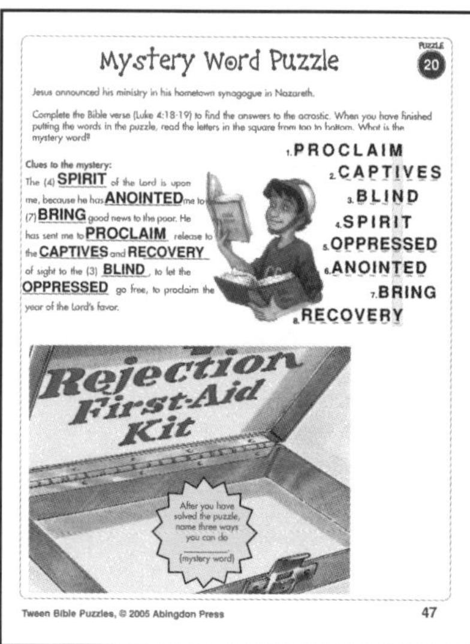

PUZZLE 20B—Color-In Puzzle

PUZZLE 21—Cross-Out Puzzle

PUZZLE 21B—Nurture Acrostic

PUZZLE 22—Choose

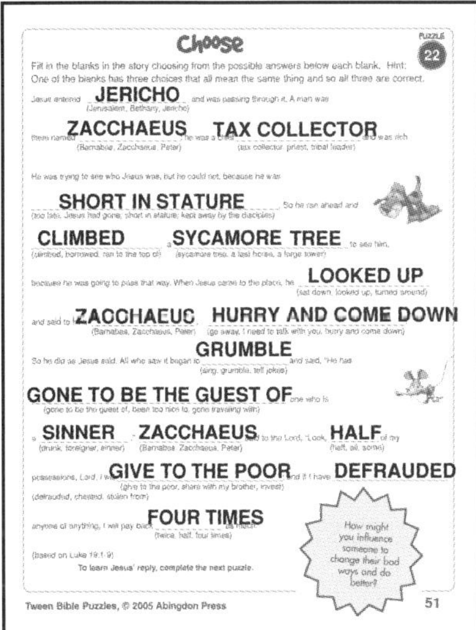

PUZZLE 22B—Word Maze

PUZZLE 23—Help Bob, Please!

<u>Peter</u> was the man who preached the first great sermon on Pentecost.

<u>Paul</u> and <u>Barnabas</u> traveled to many places together, including to Antioch.

<u>James</u> and <u>John</u> asked Jesus to put them in the greatest position.

How to work the puzzle:

1. If there are two pairs of brothers and Paul and Barnabas are NOT related, then the brothers are Andrew and Peter and James and John.

2. One pair of disciples has a brother who preached a great sermon on Pentecost. That would have to be one of the brothers from the pairs Andrew and Peter or James and John.

3. One pair traveled to many different countries to spread the good news, and another pair were favorites of Jesus. Reading Mark 10:35-37 will tell you which pair asked Jesus to put them in the greatest position. This pair would be James and John.

4. Paul was not at the Pentecost celebration and Paul and Barnabas were not brothers, so neither Paul nor Barnabas preached on Pentecost. Since James and John were the brothers who asked Jesus to put them in a great position, neither of them preached on Pentecost. That means that the preacher was either Andrew or Peter.

5. Since Andrew had a brother who was a great preacher, that would mean that Peter is the man who preached a great sermon on Pentecost.

6. Since Paul and Barnabas is the only pair that is left, by process of elimination that would make them the pair that traveled to many places together, including to Antioch.

	Brothers	Asked for Great Position	Preached	Traveled
Andrew and Peter	•	X	•	X
James and John	•	•	X	X
Paul and Barnabas	X	X	X	•

PUZZLE 23B—It's Not Hot

BUT IT IS NOT SO AMONG YOU; BUT WHOEVER WISHES TO BECOME GREAT AMONG YOU MUST BE YOUR SERVANT, AND WHOEVER WISHES TO BE FIRST AMONG YOU MUST BE SLAVE OF ALL.

PUZZLE 24—Letters of Forgiveness

FOR IF YOU FORGIVE OTHERS THEIR TRESPASSES, YOUR HEAVENLY FATHER WILL ALSO FORGIVE YOU; BUT IF YOU DO NOT FORGIVE OTHERS, NEITHER WILL YOUR FATHER FORGIVE YOUR TRESPASSES.

PUZZLE 24B—Numbers, Numbers, and Numbers

The answers to the puzzles at the top of the page will depend upon the hourly wage you select. In the following example, the hourly wage is $6.00.

Talents—In our puzzle we calculate a talent as one year's wages.
6 X 40 (number of hours in a week) X 52 (weeks in a year) X 10,000 (number of talents owed) = **124,800,000**

Denarii—A denarii is approximately one day's wages.
6 X 8 (number of hours in a day) X 100 (number of denarii owed) = **4,800**

(Because a talent was worth more than fifteen years' wages of a laborer, the difference between what the first slave owed and what the second slave owed was actually greater.)

Answer to puzzle at bottom of page:
10 x 6 = <u>60</u>
15 ÷ 3 = <u>5</u>
6 x 2 = <u>12</u>

<u>Total</u>   <u>77</u>

PUZZLE 25—Beatitude Math Puzzle

BLESSED ARE THOSE WHO ARE PERSECUTED FOR RIGHTEOUSNESS' SAKE, FOR THEIRS IS THE KINGDOM OF HEAVEN.

PUZZLE 25B—Jesus' Teachings

SERMON on the MOUNT

PUZZLE 26—Inheriting the Kingdom

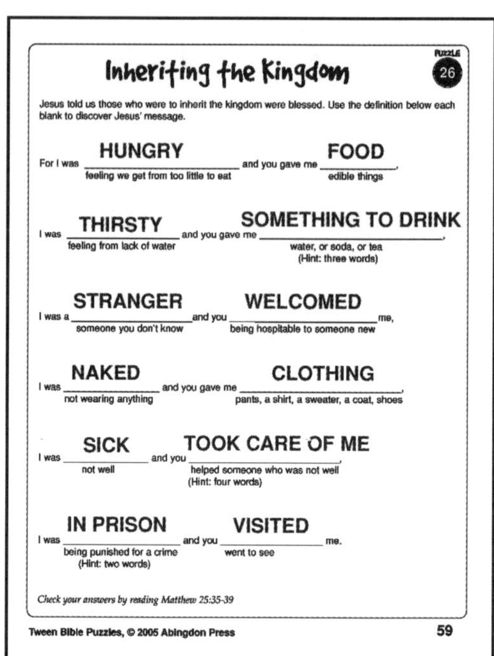

PUZZLE 26B—Out of Order

JUST AS YOU DID IT TO ONE OF THE LEAST OF THESE WHO ARE MEMBERS OF MY FAMILY, YOU DID IT TO ME.

Answers—New Testament Puzzles (Part 2)

PUZZLE 27—Some of These Words Are Not Like the Others

MY HOUSE SHALL BE CALLED A HOUSE OF PRAYER; BUT YOU ARE MAKING IT A DEN OF ROBBERS.

PUZZLE 27B—Cleansing of the Temple Maze

PUZZLE 28—Symbols of Holy Week

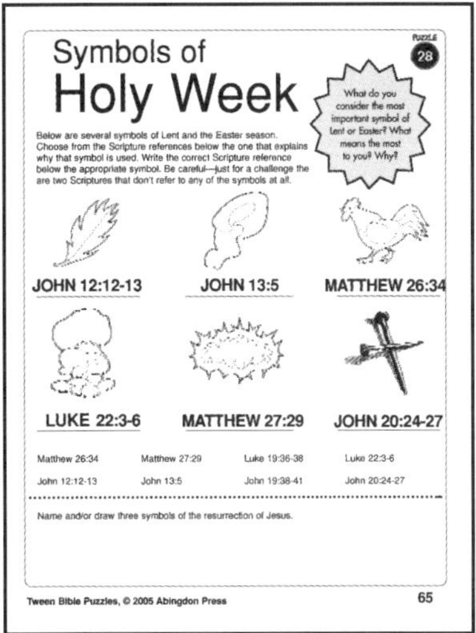

PUZZLE 28B—What Was the Example That Jesus Set?

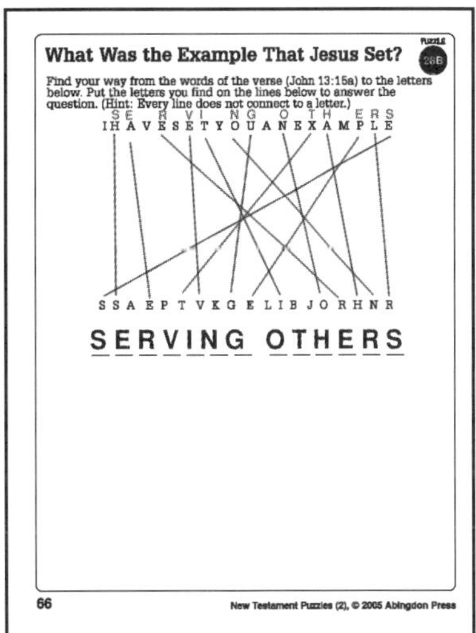

PUZZLE 29—Jesus at Prayer

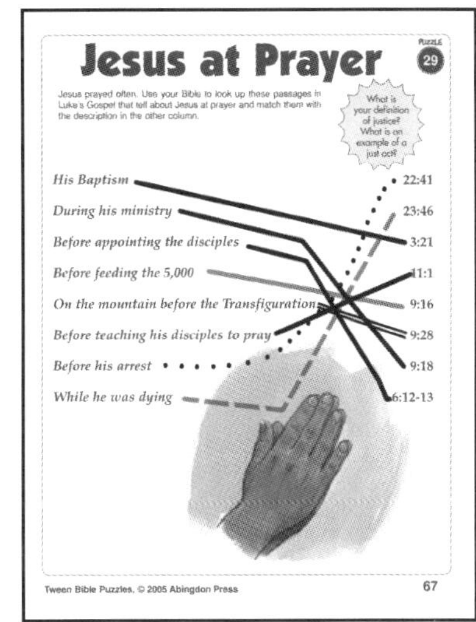

PUZZLE 29B—What Did Judas Do?

PUZZLE 30—Pilate

YOU WOULD HAVE NO POWER OVER ME UNLESS IT HAD BEEN GIVEN YOU FROM ABOVE.

PUZZLE 30B—Gather Them Up

MY KINGDOM IS NOT FROM THIS WORLD.

PUZZLE 31—Choices, Choices, Choices

1. c	5. a
2. c	6. b
3. b	7. b
4. b	

PUZZLE 31B—Tried and Sentenced

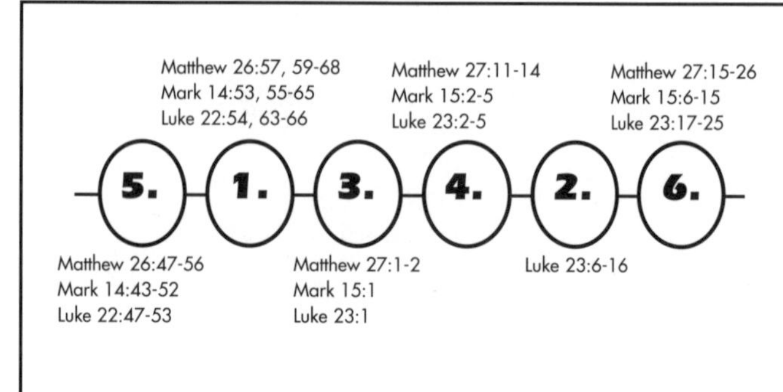

PUZZLE 32—The Promise

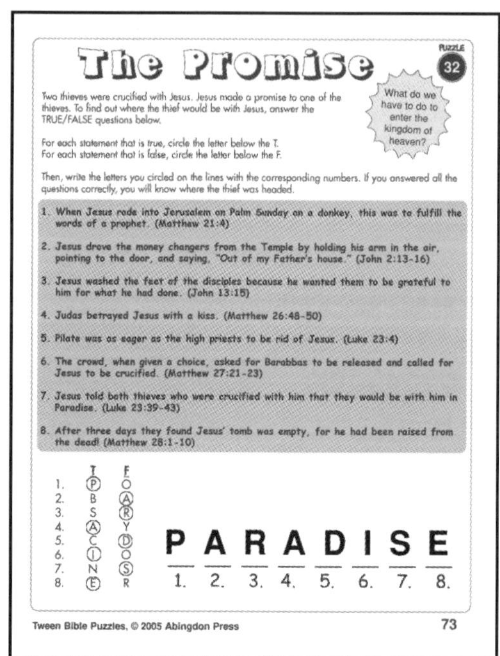

PUZZLE 32B—Who Did _______ Say That I Am?

Teacher/Leader: There are no specific answers for this puzzle—the answers are the opinions of the tweens. Allow all reasonable answers.

PUZZLE 33—Easter Crossword

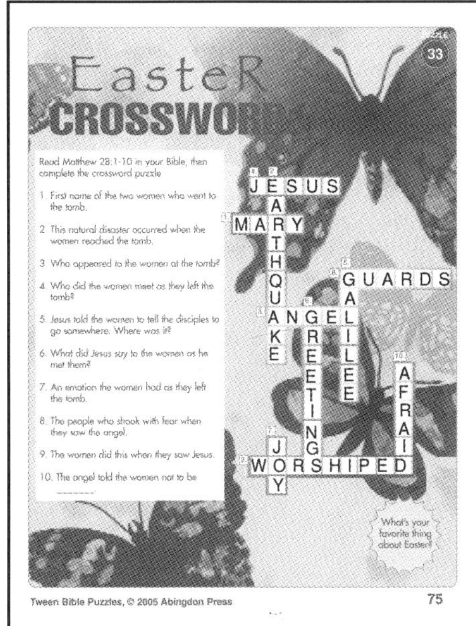

PUZZLE 33B—Scripture Logic

HE IS NOT HERE; FOR HE HAS BEEN RAISED.

Clue number 1 tells you there are only twelve letters of the alphabet used. Four of these letters are vowels. Eight of these letters are consonants. One vowel is used seven times; that means it is probably "E," the most used letter in the English language.

Clue number 3 tells you that eight consonants are used: B, D, F, H, N, R, S and T. With E being one vowel, you now know all but three of the letters, and these three are all vowels (only one vowel is not used).

Clue number 6—If the pronouns are "He," then those pronouns are two places "E" is used in the puzzle. There are five more places "E" is used.

Remember that the women were looking for Jesus at the tomb, but instead of Jesus they find an angel. What has happened? Where is Jesus? (Jesus is not here). Look at the question on the page. What does it tell them about Jesus? (For he has been raised).

PUZZLE 34—Report of the Guard

YOU WILL KNOW THE TRUTH AND THE TRUTH WILL MAKE YOU FREE.

PUZZLE 34B—Fill It In

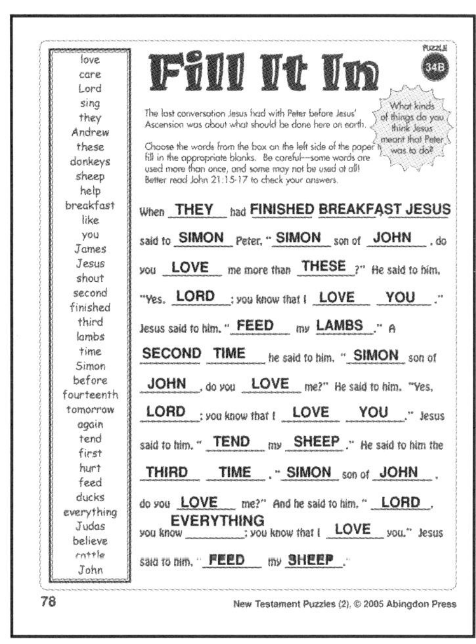

PUZZLE 35—Straight and Curvy

PENTECOST

PUZZLE 35B—Hidden Pentecost Message

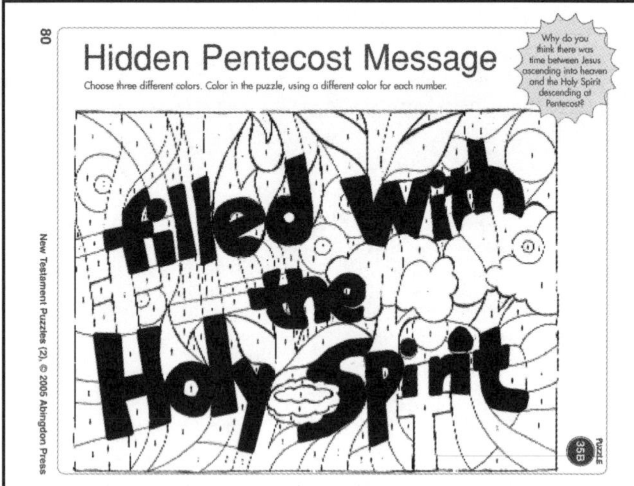

PUZZLE 36—Crack the Code

LET US WORK FOR THE GOOD OF ALL, AND ESPECIALLY FOR THOSE OF THE FAMILY OF FAITH.

There are seven people wearing "7" in the illustration.

PUZZLE 36B—An Important Number

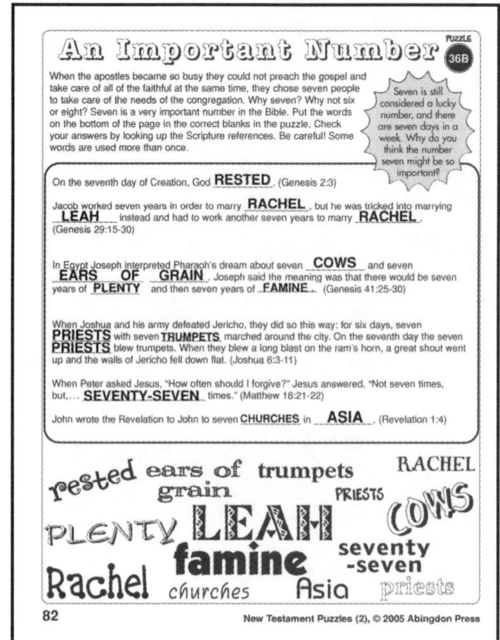

PUZZLE 37—It's in the Math

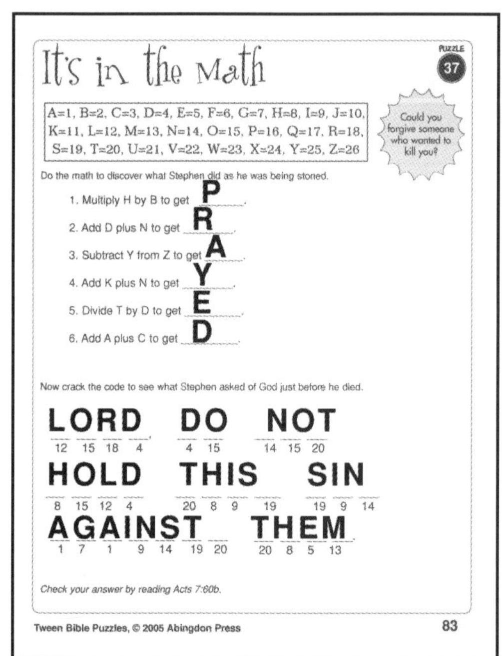

PUZZLE 37B—Name Maze

PUZZLE 38—Visit Damascus Road

1. **THREATS and MURDER**
2. **HIGH PRIEST**
3. **JERUSALEM**
4. **DAMASCUS**
5. **PERSECUTE**
6. **ANANIAS**
7. **STRAIGHT**
8. **HOLY SPIRIT**
9. **SCALES**
10. **SYNAGOGUE**

PUZZLE 38B—Crossword Puzzle

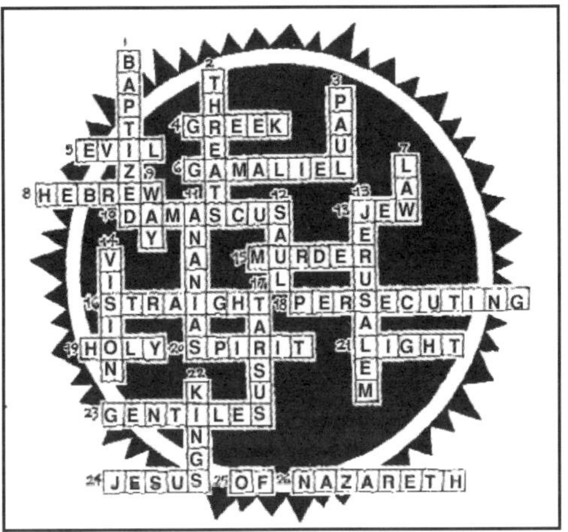

PUZZLE 39—Follow the Maze

PUZZLE 39B—Bible Story Characters

Teacher/Leader: There are no specific answers for the puzzle. Let the tweens' express their opinions—it helps them stretch their thinking. Allow all reasonable answers.

Answers—Summer Sunday School Puzzles

PUZZLE 40—A Book Discovered

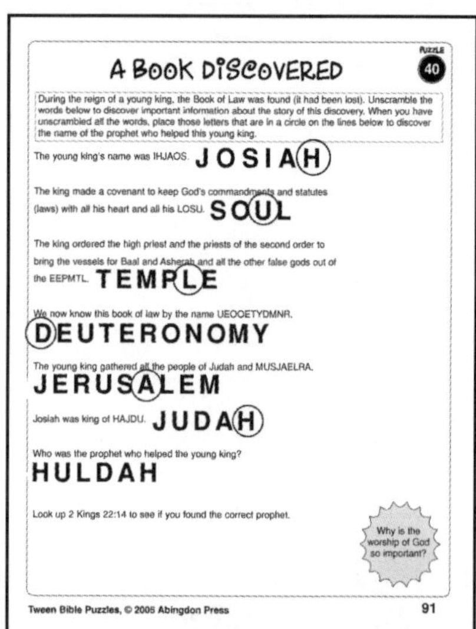

PUZZLE 40B—Josiah's Faithfulness Maze

PUZZLE 41—It's in the Code

FOR YOU SHALL GO TO ALL TO WHOM I SEND YOU, AND YOU SHALL SPEAK WHATEVER I COMMAND YOU.

PUZZLE 41B—God's Message

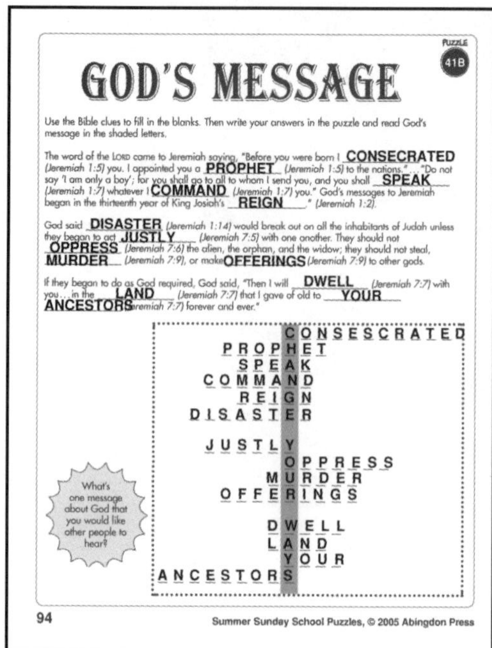

PUZZLE 42—Jonah Word Search

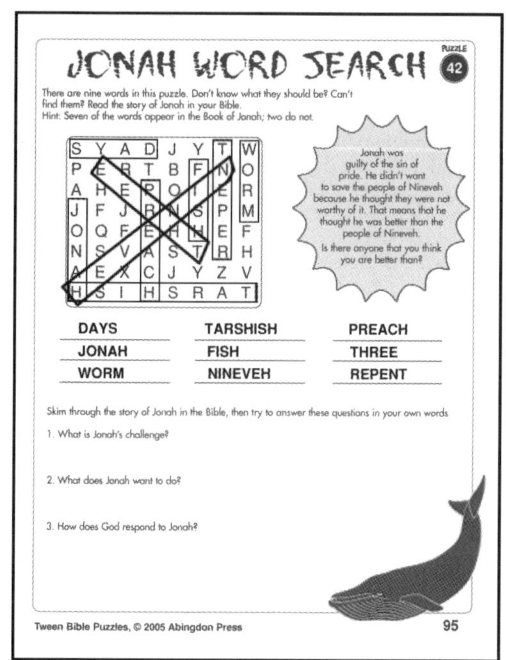

PUZZLE 42B—Crossword Puzzle

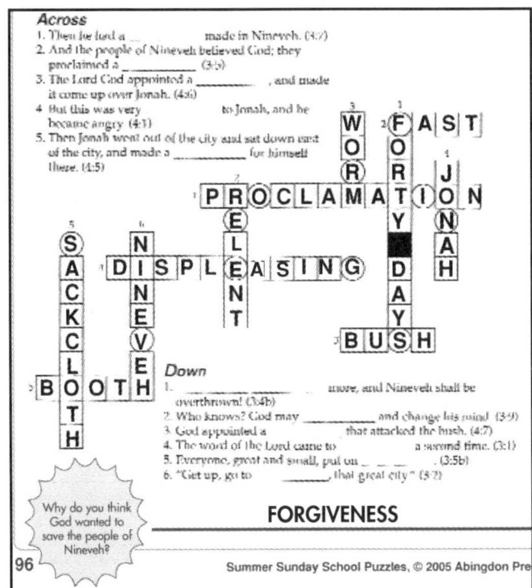

Across

1. Then he had a _____ made in Nineveh. (4:7)
2. And the people of Nineveh believed God; they proclaimed a _____ (3:5)
3. The Lord God appointed a _____, and made it come up over Jonah. (4:6)
4. But this was very _____ to Jonah, and he became angry. (4:1)
5. Then Jonah went out of the city and sat down east of the city, and made a _____ for himself there. (4:5)

Down

1. _____ more, and Nineveh shall be overthrown! (3:4b)
2. Who knows? God may _____ and change his mind. (3:9)
3. God appointed a _____ that attacked the bush. (4:7)
4. The word of the Lord came to _____ a second time. (3:1)
5. Everyone, great and small, put on _____. (3:5b)
6. "Get up, go to _____, that great city" (3:2)

FORGIVENESS

96 Summer Sunday School Puzzles, © 2005 Abingdon Press

PUZZLE 43—Who's a Prophet?

P	Isaiah	**X**	Saul—King
X	John the Baptist—New Testament Prophet	**X**	David—King
X	Matthew—Tax Collector (Apostle)	**P**	Micah
P	Jeremiah	**P**	Nathan
P	Amos	**P**	Habakkuk
P	Ezekiel	**P**	Zephaniah
X	Luke—Physician	**P**	Haggai
X	Deborah—Judge	**X**	Esther—Queen
P	Daniel	**P**	Zechariah
P	Hosea	**P**	Malachi
X	Paul—Tentmaker (Apostle)	**P**	Huldah
P	Jonah	**X**	Ruth—Gleaner
P	Joel		
X	Josiah—King		
P	Obadiah		

PUZZLE 43B—Mix and Match

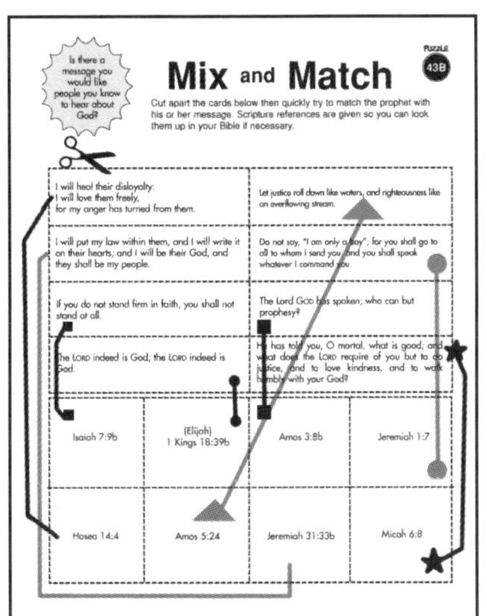

PUZZLE 44—Mixed-Up Letters

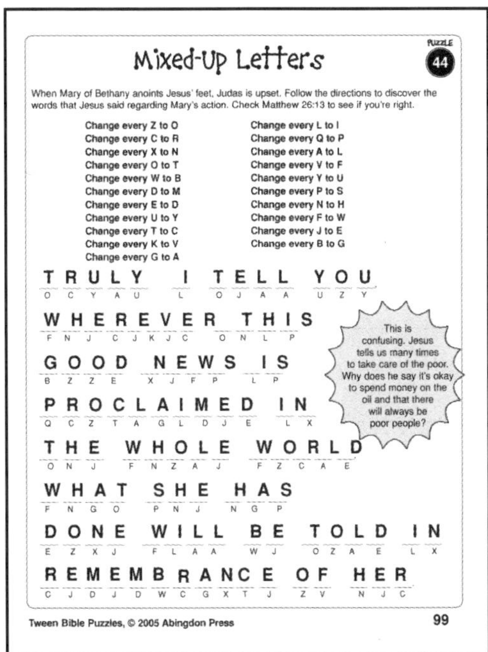

Mixed-Up Letters

When Mary of Bethany anoints Jesus' feet, Judas is upset. Follow the directions to discover the words that Jesus said regarding Mary's action. Check Matthew 26:13 to see if you're right.

Change every Z to O
Change every C to R
Change every X to N
Change every O to T
Change every W to B
Change every D to M
Change every E to D
Change every U to Y
Change every T to C
Change every K to V
Change every G to A

Change every L to I
Change every Q to P
Change every A to L
Change every V to F
Change every Y to U
Change every P to S
Change every N to H
Change every F to W
Change every J to E
Change every B to G

TRULY I TELL YOU
O C Y A U   L   O J A A   U Z Y

WHEREVER THIS
F N J C J K J C   O N L P

GOOD NEWS IS
B Z Z E   X J F P   L P

PROCLAIMED IN
Q C Z T A G L D J E   L X

THE WHOLE WORLD
O N J   F N Z A J   F Z C A E

WHAT SHE HAS
F N G O   P N J   N G P

DONE WILL BE TOLD IN
E Z X J   F L A A   W J   O Z A E   L X

REMEMBRANCE OF HER
C J D J D W C G X T J   Z V   N J C

Tween Bible Puzzles, © 2005 Abingdon Press 99

PUZZLE 44B—Gospel Comparison

Matthew 26:6-13	Mark 14:3-9	John 12:1-8
at Bethany, in the house of Simon the leper	at Bethany, in the house of Simon the lepor	at Bethany, in the house of Lazarus
sitting at the table	sitting at the table	sitting at the dinner table
		Mary of Bethany
an alabaster jar of very costly ointment	an alabaster jar of very costly ointment of nard	a pound of costly perfume made of pure nard
poured the ointment on Jesus' head	broke open the jar and poured the ointment on Jesus' head	anointed Jesus' feet and wiped them with her hair
"Why this waste? For this ointment could have been sold for a large sum, and the money given to the poor."	"Why was the ointment wasted in this way? For this ointment could have been sold for more than three hundred denarii, and the money given to the poor."	"Why was this perfume not sold for three hundred denarii and the money given to the poor?"
a large sum	more than three hundred denarii	three hundred denarii
"Why do you trouble the woman? She has performed a good service for me....By pouring this ointment on my body she has prepared me for burial."	"Let her alone; why do you trouble her? She has performed a good service for me. For you always have the poor with you,...but you will not always have me...."	"Leave her alone. She bought it so that she might keep it for the day of my burial. You always have the poor with you, but you do not always have me."
what the woman did for Jesus	what the woman did for Jesus	

YOUR SINS ARE FORGIVEN.

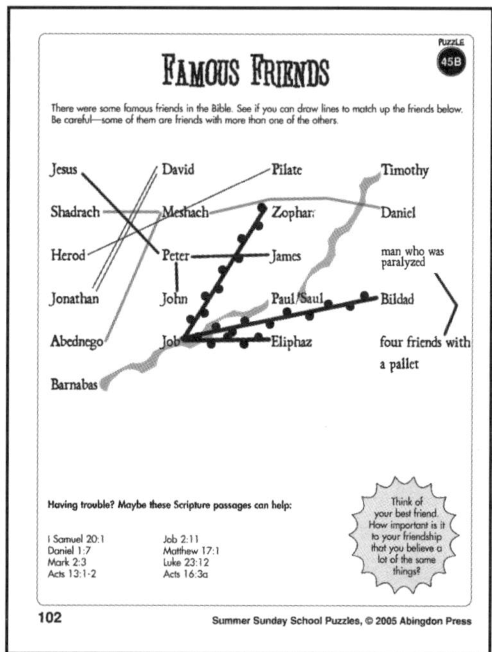

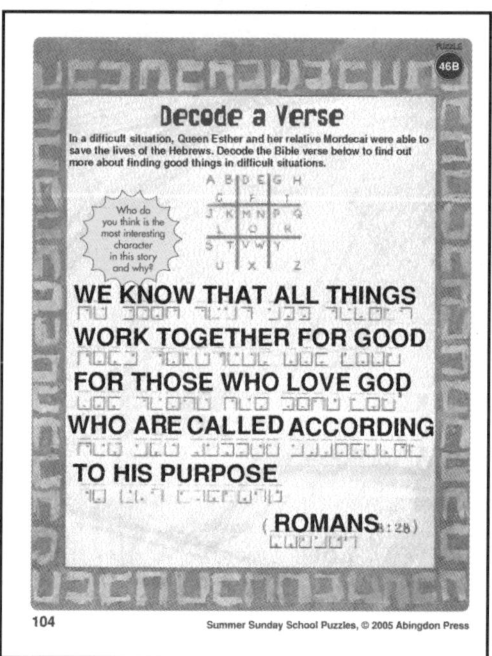

LET ME BE WEIGHED IN A JUST BALANCE, AND LET GOD KNOW MY INTEGRITY!

PUZZLE 47B—In a Swirl

WHERE WERE YOU WHEN I LAID THE FOUNDATION OF THE EARTH?

PUZZLE 48—Daniel 6:16b

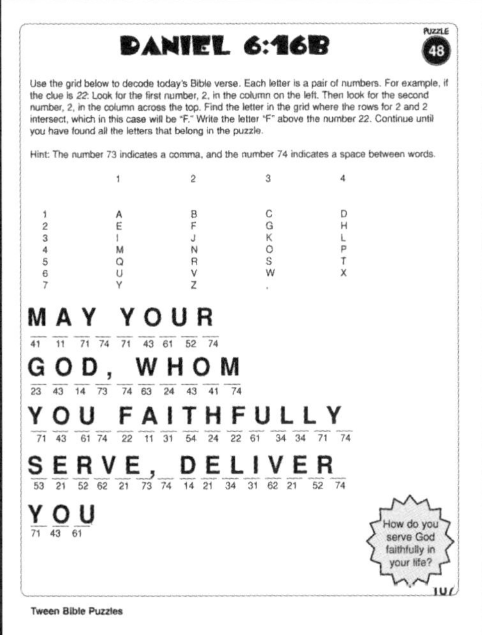

PUZZLE 48B—Testing of Faith

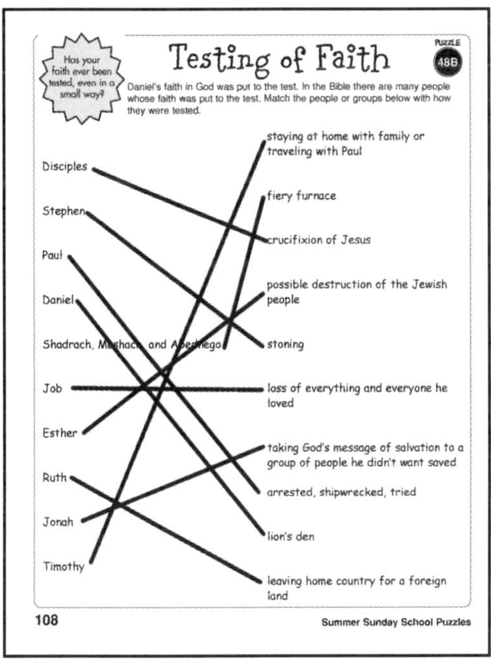

PUZZLE 49—Abigail, Peacemaker

Nabal owned **three thousand** sheep and **one thousand** goats. (1 Samuel 25:2)

David sent **ten** young men to greet Nabal. (1 Samuel 25:5)

David also strapped on his sword; and about **four hundred** men went up after David, while **two hundred** remained with the baggage. (1 Samuel 25:13)

But **one** of the young men told Abigail, Nabal's wife. (1 Samuel 25:14)

Then Abigail hurried and took **two hundred** loaves, **two** skins of wine, **five** sheep ready dressed, **five** measures of parched grain, **one hundred** clusters of raisins, and **two hundred** cakes of figs. (1 Samuel 25:18)

For as surely as the Lord the God of Israel lives, who has restrained me from hurting you, unless you had hurried and come to meet me, truly by morning there would not have been left to Nabal so much as **one** male. (1 Samuel 25:34)

PUZZLE 49B—Use Your Bible

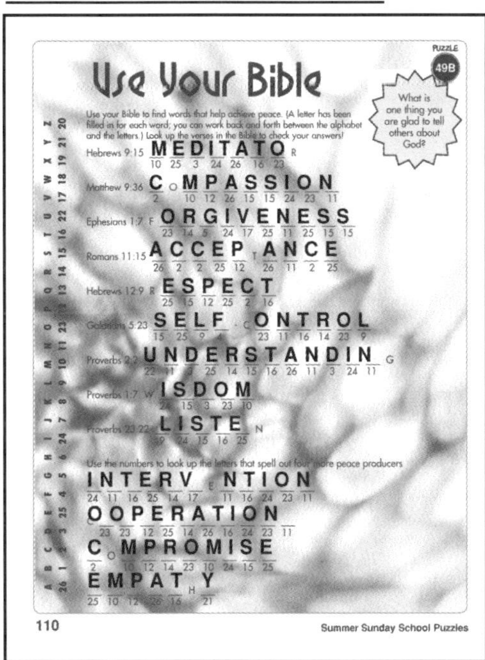

PUZZLE 50—Amos 5:24

LET JUSTICE ROLL DOWN LIKE WATERS, AND RIGHTEOUSNESS LIKE AN EVER-FLOWING STREAM.

PUZZLE 50B—What Doesn't Belong

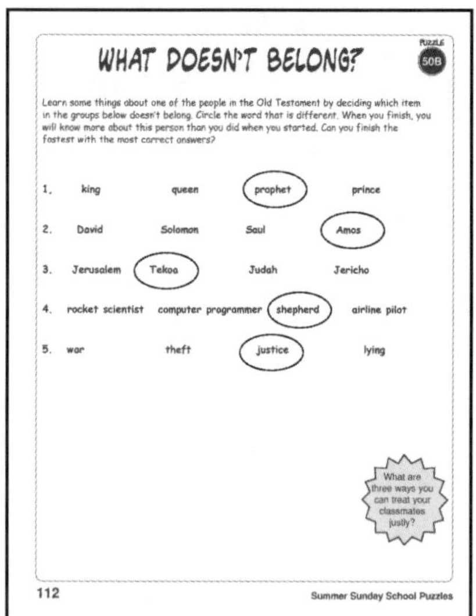

PUZZLE 51—Micah's Poem

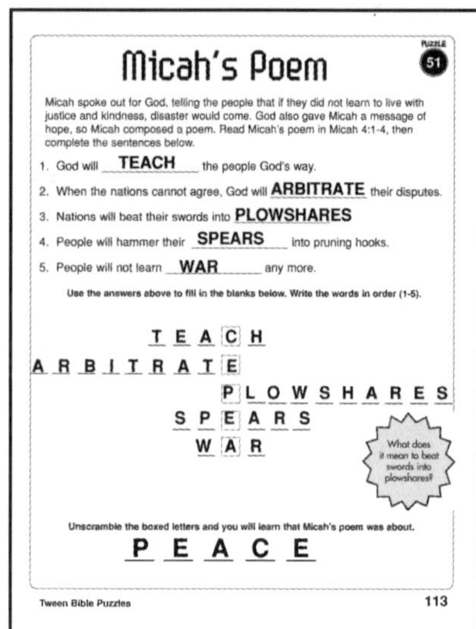

PUZZLE 51B—Match the Word With the Meaning

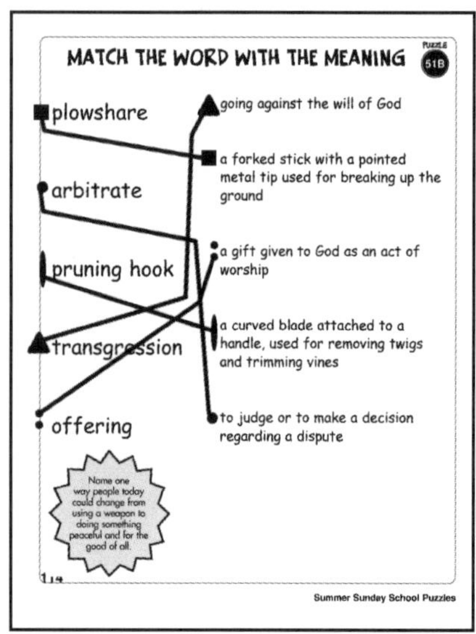

PUZZLE 52—Jesus' Words About Justice

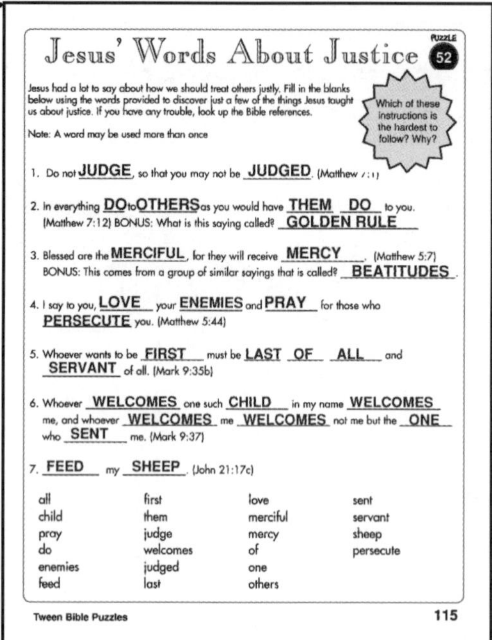

PUZZLE 52B—Building Stones for Life

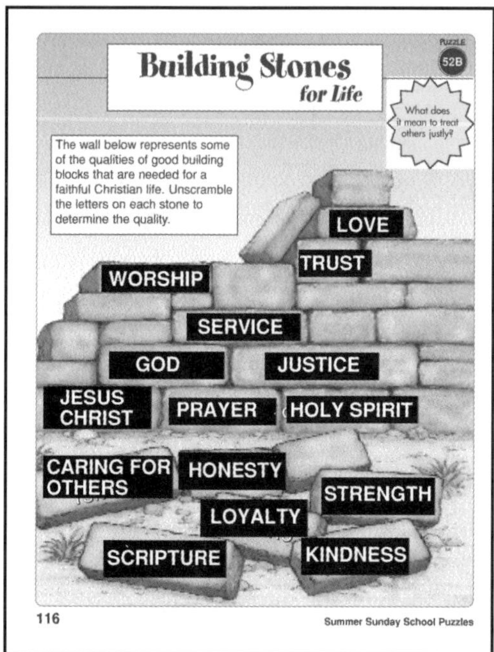

Puzzle Answers

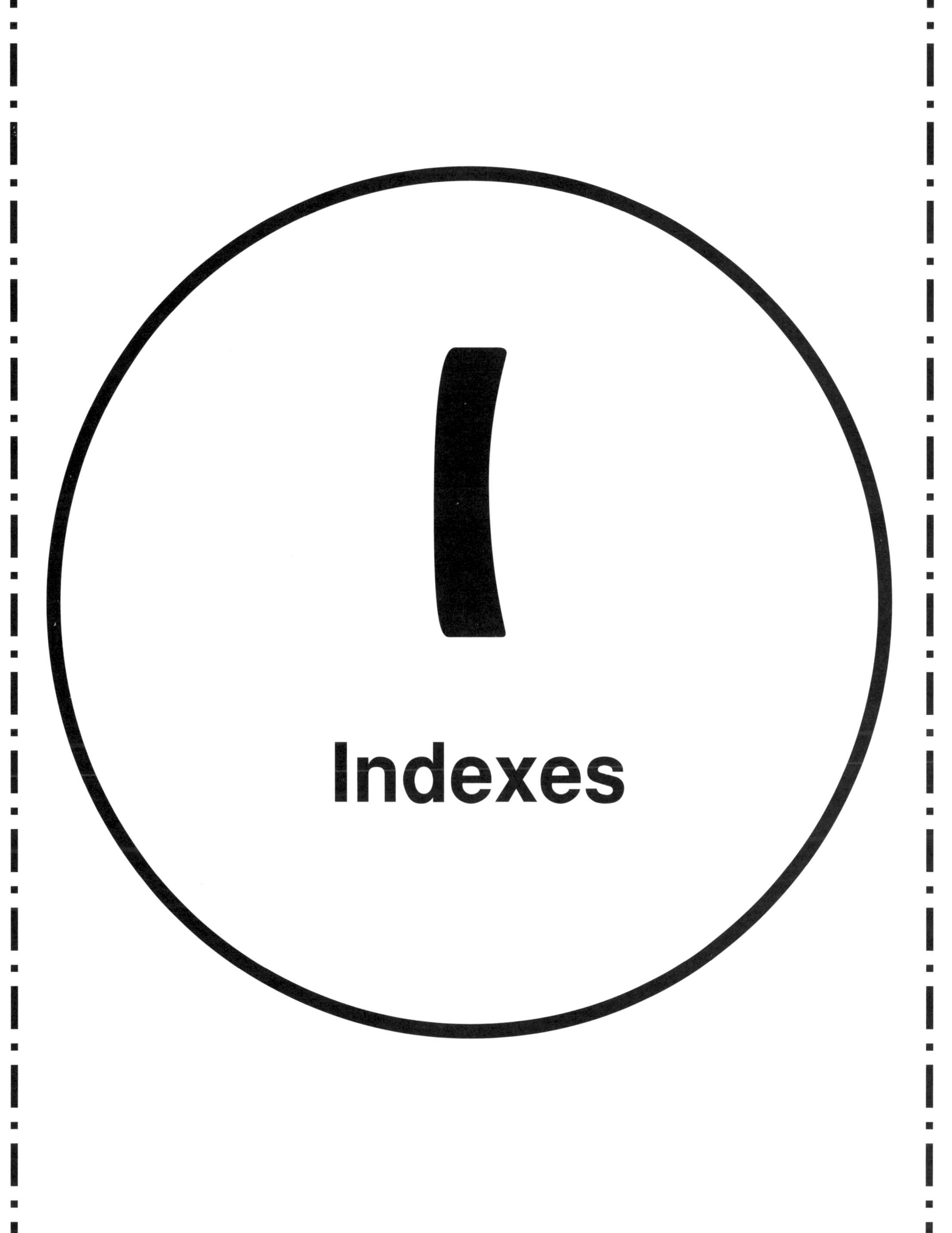
I
Indexes

Topical Index

Scripture Index

**Additional Puzzles for Summer Sessions

Mixed New Testament Scripture References

Note: Building Stones for Life (Faith Words)—not related to any specific Scripture.

**Additional Puzzles for Summer Sessions

Credits

pp. 7-9: *Exploring Faith: Preteen* Student Fall 2000, © 2000 Cokesbury.

pp. 13, 14, 16: *New Invitation: Grades 5-6* Student Fall 1997, © 1994, 1997 Cokesbury.

p. 19: *Exploring Faith: Preteen* Student Summer 2004, © 2004 Cokesbury.

pp. 20, 93, 95: *Exploring Faith: Preteen* Student Fall 2001, © 2001 Cokesbury.

p. 22: *New Invitation: Grades 5-6* Student Fall 1999, © 1996, 1999 Cokesbury.

pp. 26, 37, 41: *Exploring Faith: Preteen* Student Winter 2002-2003, © 2002 Cokesbury.

p. 28: *Exploring Faith: Older Elementary* Student Fall 2003, © 2003 Cokesbury.

p. 36: *Exploring Faith: Bible Brain Pak* Summer 2004, © 2004 Cokesbury.

pp. 38, 46, 48: *One Room Sunday School Reproducible Activities* Winter 2004-2005, © 2004 Abingdon Press.

pp. 42, 47, 100, 101: *Exploring Faith: Preteen* Student Winter 2001-2002, © 2001 Cokesbury.

p. 49: *BibleZone: Older Elementary #10,* © 2000 Abingdon Press.

p. 50: *One Room Sunday School Reproducible Activities* Winter 2002-2003, © 2002 Abingdon Press.

pp. 57, 92: *Exploring Faith: Preteen* Student Fall 2002, © 2002 Cokesbury.

pp. 64, 74, 78: *Exploring Faith: Preteen* Student Spring 2003, © 2002 Cokesbury.

p. 65: *Symbols of Faith,* © 2001 Abingdon Press.

p. 67: *One Room Sunday School Reproducible Activities* Spring 2004, © 2003 Abingdon Press.

pp. 72, 84: *Exploring Faith: Preteen* Student Spring 2001, © 2000 Cokesbury.

p. 75: *New Invitation: Grades 5-6* Student Spring 1999, © 1995, 1998 Cokesbury.

pp. 79, 88: *Exploring Faith: Preteen* Student Spring 2002, © 2001 Cokesbury.

p. 80: *One Room Sunday School Reproducible Activities* Summer 2001, © 2001 Abingdon Press.

p. 81: *BibleZone: Older Elementary #11,* © 1999 Abingdon Press.

p. 85: *Exploring Faith: Preteen* Student Spring 2004, © 2003 Cokesbury.

p. 86: *One Room Sunday School Reproducible Activities* Spring 2004, © 2003 Abingdon Press; text by James Ritchie, © 1996 Cokesbury.

p. 87: *One Room Sunday School Reproducible Activities* Spring 2002, © 2001 Abingdon Press.

p. 94: *New Invitation: Grades 5-6* Summer 1995, © 1995 Cokesbury.

pp. 96, 104: *New Invitation: Grades 5-6* Summer 2000, © 1997, 2000 Cokesbury.

pp. 103, 109, 110, 114, 116: *Exploring Faith: Preteen* Student Summer 2002, © 2002 Cokesbury.

p. 105: *One Room Sunday School Reproducible Activities* Summer 2003, © 2003 Abingdon Press.

p. 113: *New Invitation: Grades 5-6* Summer 1998, © 1995, 1998 Cokesbury.

Art and Photo Credits

p. 1: Ron Benedict

p. 7 (top of page): Dennis Jones, © 2000 Cokesbury; (bottom of page): Roger Payne/Linden Artists, © 2005 Cokesbury.

pp. 8-9: Mary Reaves, © 2000 Cokesbury.

p. 10: © BrandXphotos.

p. 13: Marvin Jarboe, © 1997 Cokesbury.

p. 19: Randy Wollenmann, © 2004 Cokesbury.

p. 20: Corbin Hillam, © 2001 Cokesbury.

p. 24: Dennis Jones, © 2004 Cokesbury.

p. 27: Jim Padgett, © 2003 Cokesbury.

p. 28: Randy Wollenmann, © 2003 Cokesbury.

p. 29: Paige Easter, © 2005 Cokesbury.

p. 32: Dennis Jones, © 2004 Cokesbury.

p. 36: Robert S. Jones, © 2004 Cokesbury.

p. 37: Doug Jones, © 2002 Cokesbury.

p. 38: Brenda Gilliam, © 2004 Abingdon Press.

p. 40: Bill Ross, © 2004 Cokesbury.

p. 42: Pat Binder, © 2001 Cokesbury.

p. 46: Nell Fisher, © 2004 Abingdon Press.

p. 47: (top of page) Mary Reaves, © 2000 Cokesbury; (bottom of page) Nell Fisher © 2000 Cokesbury.

p. 48: Brenda Gilliam, © 2004 Abingdon Press.

p. 49: Jim Padgett, © 1999 Abingdon Press.

p. 50: Corbin Hillam, © 2002 Abingdon Press.

p. 52: Paige Easter, © 2005 Cokesbury.

p. 54 (top of page): Randy Wollenmann; (bottom of page): Keitha Vincent.

p. 63: Rubberball Productions.

p. 64: Dennis Jones, © 2002 Cokesbury.

p. 65: Florence Davis, © 2001 Abingdon Press.

p. 66: Keitha Vincent.

p. 67: Dick Wahl, © 2002 Cokesbury.

p. 71: Keitha Vincent.

p. 75: Cheryl Mendenhall, © 1996 Cokesbury.

p. 80: Robert S. Jones, © 2001 Abingdon Press.

p. 81: Jim Padgett, © 2000 Abingdon Press.

p. 84: Robert S. Jones, © 2000 Cokesbury.

p. 85: Big Cheese Photos.

p. 86: Dennis Jones, © 2003 Abingdon Press.

p. 87: Megan Jeffery, © 1998 Abingdon Press.

p. 88: Creatas.

p. 92: Dennis Jones, © 2002 Cokesbury.

p. 93: Big Cheese Photos.

p. 101: Doug Jones, © 2001 Cokesbury.

p. 102: Bill Ross, © 2005 Cokesbury.

p. 103: Corbin Hillam, © 2002 Cokesbury.

p. 104: Randy Wollenmann, © 1997, 2000 Cokesbury.

p. 105: Susan Harrison, © 2003 Abingdon Press.

p. 106: Paige Easter, © 2005 Abingdon Press.

p. 112: Creatas.

p. 116: Randy Wollenmann, © 2002 Cokesbury.